2018/99610

Voodoo Shit for Men

Library and Archives Canada Cataloguing in Publication

Bisson-Somerville, Michèle, 1970-, author
    Voodoo shit for men : flex your intuitive muscle / Michèle
Bisson-Somerville.

ISBN 978-1-77141-068-7 (pbk.)

1. Intuition. I. Title.

BF315.5.B47 2014   153.4'4   C2014-905132-8

Voodoo Shit for Men

Flex your Intuitive Muscle

Trust your intuitive muscle, michèle

Michèle Bisson-Somerville

Book Cover Design: Marla Thompson
Typeset: Greg Salisbury
Photographer: Alanna Milaney: www.alannamilaney.com

DISCLAIMER: This is a work of non-fiction. The information in this
book reflects the opinions of Michèle Bisson-Somerville. Readers of this
publication agree that neither Michèle Bisson-Somerville nor her publisher
will be held responsible or liable for damages that may be alleged or resulting directly or indirectly from their use of this publication. The names of
the clients and hospital staff have been changed to protect their privacy and
confidentiality. All external links are provided as a resource only and are not
guaranteed to remain active for any length of time. Neither the publisher
nor the author can be held accountable for the information provided by, or
actions resulting from accessing these resources.

To my three sons—may your intuitive muscles stay strong. You are my inspiration!

I dedicate this to all my heroes—all the men in the world!
You are your own heroes!

Testimonials

"Most of us are unsure of our 'gut instinct,' we waffle, second guess and too often lament over decisions of all types. It is often said there is no such thing as a bad decision, because who would make a decision they knew to be bad for themselves on purpose? Michèle Bisson-Somerville shares her insights and truth about dealing with these issues in this critical area of intuition, sharing her tools for both business and life!"
Mark E. Sackett, President/Creative Director/Executive Producer/Director/Public Speaker

"Thanks to Michèle Bisson-Somerville—she has an amazing way of explaining the mystery of intuition in a man's world and language. Practical and simple is powerful!"
Frank Penko, Business Owner, Impala Transport Inc.

"Having created a life where I could explore more of who I am as a man, I can't say enough about discovering the value of my own 'Voodoo Shit.' For any man looking to experience all aspects of life on a higher plane, Michèle's book will help the warrior in you come to a deeper, more illuminated experience of life by learning to flex and respond to your 'masculine intuitive muscle!'"
Doug Barlow, Network Marketing Professional, Outdoor Adventurer

"*Imagine what our world would be like if more men learned about the power of their intuition. A courageous female author, Michèle Bisson-Somerville invites men on a journey to discover their true and natural power source. The timing of this book could not be any better! More and more men are seeking an easier route. For generations we have struggled along this hike with our stubborn and competitive ego. Now we are ready to walk in harmony with our intuitive self and the first step is for us to open this book. I did and I am very grateful to learn from this intuitive author!*"

Bobby O'Neal (aka Dr. Love), RLM, Author of *Dr. Love's Prescription for a Romantic Loving Man*

Acknowledgements

This book has been brewing for many years and I am forever grateful that it has now surfaced. I feel as if I am at the Academy Awards and about to deliver my acceptance speech. There are so many people I want to thank but not enough pages to do so.

To my Grandpapa (Pèpère Bisson), thank you for all those magical evenings rocking and sitting on the front porch of your house in Welland, Ontario, learning from your intuitive wisdom. Thank you for your continued visits from the spirit world.

To my beautiful sister, Christine, who I adore so much because you have taught me to step out of my comfort zone, thank you for always believing and supporting everything I do. You are a strong woman!

To my most trusted friend, Ian—you are my older brother from another mother. I love and cherish you for never judging me and always respecting me.

To my parents, who never once told me that what I saw, heard, or felt, was not real (when I asked)—you gave me the confidence to know that what I experienced was true despite you not knowing what was going on in my world.

To my publisher, Julie, thank you for giving me the space and time to finally write this book. I am also grateful for your patience during all those years when I used to say I wasn't ready, because when I was, the process flowed quickly.

To my wonderful editor, Nina, thank you for the fabulous work in making the manuscript flow properly and helping me expand my thoughts into a clearer message.

To my three sons, Ross, Maxwell and Théodore, thank you for being patient when I hogged the computer to work on my book, and, most importantly, for all that you have taught me about flexing my intuitive muscle through your own. Keep those muscles strong and flexed. Yes, just like your abs!

To my husband, Tim, who has pissed me off beyond belief and yet who I continue to love, thank you for believing in my truth even though you could have easily disbelieved. Also, thank you for sharing your story of your personal experience during your "time-out".

To SPA DIVINE at the Inlet, thank you for the wonderful makeup application for the photo shoot. You made me look fabulous!

To all of my friends and other family members, I am grateful for your love and support.

To the entire staff at Peace Arch and Abbotsford Regional hospitals, who took care of my husband and our family during his stay in February 2013—thank you.

To all the men in my life who have come and gone, thank you for teaching me the ins and outs of your language and lifestyle, and for accepting me as part of your gang.

To all the spirits of my family and friends from beyond who continue to give me guidance each and every day—I welcome your visits!

Contents

FOREWORD

True friendship is a rare blessing in life. Sure, we can all look back and recall several friendships we have had over time. Some are childhood buddies, some are from high school or university, and others are work or neighbourhood acquaintances. What is rare is a friendship that lasts a lifetime—one that bridges both time and geography. This is the kind of friend that, no matter what stage of life you are at, how far away you may live, or how long it has been since you spoke, is always there and it is as if no time has passed. Rarer still is when that friend is of the opposite sex.

For close to 30 years I have had such a friend in Michèle Bisson-Somerville. This friendship happened rather by chance, meeting her through my girlfriend at the time. Michèle and her boyfriend had invited her to go to a U2 concert, when my girlfriend ended up with a scheduling conflict and suggested I go in her place. Fortunately my desire to see the concert out-weighed my reluctance to be a third wheel with two perfect strangers that I had never met. Upon meeting Michèle for the first time there was something intuitively familiar about her and we immediately clicked. It was like we had known each other for years and we had a fabulous time together, something Michèle's boyfriend seemed to take some exception to, not really being overly comfortable with her getting along so well with another guy. Needless to say Michèle's relationship with the boyfriend ended a short time after, ushering in a new chapter in her life.

At the time, Michèle lived about an hour from where I lived and with the new free time being single, she would come to visit my girlfriend much more frequently. This allowed us to get to know each other, absent the noise and hysteria of a concert. It was during one of these trips that Michèle was introduced to one of my best buddies, Tim. Quite literally it was love at first sight. The four of us spent the summer together having a great time getting to know each other and Michèle quickly became my adopted little sister. Her fun loving, free spirited and down-to-earth way made her an instant friend with all the other buddies we hung out with. It was like she had been part of our lives for years and was just one of the guys. She just seemed to "get" us and felt totally comfortable in a male-dominated circle of friends.

I was unaware of the depth of our friendship until my relationship with my girlfriend, Michèle's best friend, ended. Devastated at the time, I saw my world crumbling and would have expected that I may also lose my "little sister" in the process, assuming it would be weird for her to still want to hang out with me while still being close to my now "ex-girlfriend." But just the opposite happened—we became closer friends. Michèle was there to listen and lend a shoulder. Genuinely kind and caring by nature, she truly helped me through what, at the time, was one of the lowest points in my life.

Nothing gave me greater joy than to watch Tim and Michèle's relationship grow and strengthen. One of my proudest and most memorable moments was standing up at their wedding as they set off on their life together as husband and wife. I admired their relationship. It was like they were truly meant to be together. In my mind they were simply "Tim & Michèle," and then there was everybody else.

I have always been inspired by Michèle's unyielding drive and her ability to give of herself. From being a university graduate and pursuing a successful 15-year career in the corporate world, to raising three beautiful boys and supporting their various interests and hobbies, her passion and caring for others has been endless. No matter what seems to be going on in her life, Michèle always makes you feel like you have her full attention and is willing to, yet again, give of herself to lend an ear or help in any way she can.

Although I have known Michèle for these past 30 years, having shared some of our most joyous and tragic life experiences, there is another side of Michèle that I, in fact, did not know about. As it turns out, not too many other people walking this earth know about it either. This would be Michèle's strong sense of intuition and clairvoyance. She has kept this side hidden from the world partly due to her journey of discovering these gifts for herself and also because she has been exploring the best way in which to reveal these gifts to the people around her.

I am both thrilled and honoured to be asked by Michèle to announce that, at long last, this journey has come to an end with the release of her first book. In the pages that follow, Michèle will take you down a path of self-discovery by sharing stories from her life. This journey will cover some of her most joyful times with her three beautiful boys, to anguishing moments as her husband Tim fought for his life in a coma. Along the way, Michèle will share her intuitive talents and techniques to allow you, the reader, to harness the intuitive talents you naturally possess.

In only a way Michèle can, she continues to have an insatiable desire to give of herself and help others in the process. This, coupled with her intuitive ability to connect with the male friends in her life, is the genesis of this book. After 30 years of knowing Michèle I am excited to get to know her a little bit better through this book and am proud to introduce my dear and trusted friend to you.

Ian Morin, Lifelong Friend

Introduction

Why are this book and my work as your personal intuitive trainer so important to me? As a mother of three boys and for all the men in this world, my passion, my work is for you to recognize that you have a superpower that is out of this world! Don't let anyone—even yourself—tell you otherwise! It is crucial and vitally important for you to understand your superpower: use it, own it, and flex it! Intuition doesn't only belong to women! You, too, have an incredible power.

In this book, you'll learn how to recognize it, hear it, see it, feel it, know it, and respect it. Throughout my clients' stories, my personal journey, what I observe from my three boys and my husband's transformation, you will be able to relate to and learn from what others have experienced. You will also notice throughout these intimate stories, how the intuitive muscle can be blocked, damaged, doubted, and sometimes feared. Then miraculously, the lights go on and presto, just like magic, your "inner voice" is full force; the fire within your gut is ignited, and the web in your "spidey-senses" is bang on. I want every man to master his own Voodoo power. Do not allow others to take it away from you. Do not let others tell you that it only belongs to women. It is imperative that you accept the power you already have. Together, let's spark your inner fire!

I have been around men my whole life and now, as a mother of boys, I want them and you to know that this is your time to step up, too. Become more aware, use your powers of observation, and be more conscious. I never want my boys to allow their gut instincts—their intuition—to fade or for the flame to burn out. I do not want yours to either, hence the reason for this book, Voodoo Shit for Men, Flex Your Intuitive Muscle, and my work with Voodoo Shit for Men (voodooshitformen.com) and Spiritual Ventures (spiritualventures.ca).

Look around the bookshelves, peek into a yoga class, a meditation class; what do you see? Women, women, women... Where are all the good men, I ask you? Where are you? Hopefully, you'll be sitting on my couch one day soon or in a room full of other men discussing how your superpower—your intuitive muscle—came in handy. I want you to have a place you can call your own to flex your intuition, to tap into your spidey-senses, and use your X-ray vision to change your life! So sit back, relax, and let's have fun!

By the way, you'll come across "Michèleisms" throughout this book. A "Michèleism" is a commonly used English expression that I screw up and put a twist on. I mark all Michèleisms with an asterisk on either side of *the term*.

Michèleism examples include *Sky rises*, *Ninth Cloud*, *Peanutting comments*, *Perfusing like a pig*.

Part One
My Secret Identity

The Background—Why Listen to Me?

"I don't think I ever thought of myself as Superman. But there were people who thought of me that way, and maybe I believed them a little."
Eminem

Two thousand thirteen was my worst year ever; 2013 had so many challenges; 2013 sucked; 2013 was the shits. I have heard this so many times from my clients. Guess what? *No Shit, Einstein*! Mine too; so now what?

Two thousand fourteen is here: a new day, a new chapter, a new year. So suck it up, boys, and let's move on. At times, that's easier said than done. So far, 2014 is pretty darn good, for my clients and me included.

The Boys and Me

So why listen to me? I am a woman who has been surrounded by boys and men my whole life. Growing up, I considered myself a tomboy. Even as a young girl in elementary school, my three best friends were boys. We used to call ourselves "The Four Musketeers." We did everything together: walk to school, eat lunch, play with "army-men," build forts, and construct rockets. I truly enjoyed spending time with my "boy" friends. They were uncomplicated, they were honest, they were to the point, and I always knew where I stood with them. I was part of the gang.

As we grew older, still hanging out, some of the girls were jealous of the relationship I had with the boys. This caused some grief in my life. Other girls often beat me up. Once the boys became aware, they became my protectors. I felt safe and accepted with them as opposed to with some of the girls.

By the time we went to high school, my gang—"The Four Musketeers"—had split up. Two of the boys went to different schools, and the other one started to hang out more with other guys. I felt a little alone, yet I maintained a positive outlook that high school would be different.

I began hanging out with some of the girls a bit more often and befriended a small group of them while still maintaining friendships with other boys. Once again, I was faced with similar situations with other girls, minus the fights that had occurred in elementary school. I was occasionally bullied, teased, and not welcomed by girls. The boys on the hand were accepting of our platonic friendships; they were not jealous that I had other "boy" friends. As young girls grew up into teenage girls, I found they got meaner. The "perceived" friendships that I had with boys were completely different from the "real" relationship. "My boys" regularly came to my defence and had to justify that "Michèle" was indeed just one of the boys, especially to their girlfriends. This generally didn't go down very well with the girls and I, in turn, would sometimes lose my "boy" friends. Holding my head high, I persevered on through high school, fitting in where I could.

Added to the mix was my highly sensitive, rock hard, flexible intuitive muscle, because it made me really different. I sensed many emotions other people felt, I saw things that others did not see, and I had a natural curiosity to discover more of this supernatural world that surrounds us; yet I kept most of it to myself. As a young child, I dabbled with my intuition by experimenting with or on a few friends. More on this later. For now, let's get back to talking about my rapport with men.

I met my most trusted, my best friend (you guessed it—a guy) in my later years of high school. Ironically, he was then dating one of my girlfriends from my childhood. He is my rock, my go-to when I need advice, my big brother. My girlfriend had moved away from my hometown when we were in second grade. We had maintained a friendship because our grandparents and our parents were long-time friends. Since our families still kept in touch with one another, we did too. All three of us even went to university together in a city midway between both our hometowns. Through my best friends, I found a new gang to hang with. He and I have now been best friends for almost thirty years, despite being separated by provinces and time. When we pick up the phone or see each other, it is just like it was yesterday. Despite sharing many thoughts, feelings, and stories with him, I never revealed my secret intuitive identity.

My Corporate Life

After graduating with a Political Science degree, I went on to work in a large, international corporation. I quickly climbed the corporate ladder and found myself in the operations department, working in the field. At the time, I was the only woman in the field, plus I was in my early twenties. The men in the operations department and I worked well together. They appreciated having a different point of view for solving challenges. This is where my intuition came into play. My supervisor would tell me, "I don't know how you know, Michèle. Just be wise and get me the proof you need to make this happen."

I always did.

Most of the storeowners that I oversaw were men in their late forties to early fifties and of European descent. I quickly gained their trust and they had confidence in my abilities in assisting them to manage their stores with record-breaking profits. Excelling in the operations field, I was named Operations Manager of the Month and Operations Manager of the Year in 1994 for achieving and exceeding my goals in business. I never questioned if I would fit in or be respected. I just knew I would be. I guess all those earlier years of hanging out with the boys came in handy. I know how men tick; I understand their language and, most importantly, I use my "spidey-senses," my gut instincts, and my intuition daily when interacting with them.

After a few years of working in the hardcore corporate world, I decided to start a family with my husband whom I had met through my male best friend. I took a bit of time off, had my three sons (did you see that coming?), and then went back to the workforce. I stuck to what I knew best and started working for a different international company in the field. Once again, I was surrounded by men. Repeating a bit of history, I moved around the field, turning almost bankrupt stores into $1-million-plus stores, while earning myself the prestigious award of Manager of the Quarter, three quarters in a row, followed by Manager of the Year in 2005. I trusted my instincts and they guided me my whole career in business, hence, accelerating my success in the corporate world. Besides, I was playing with the big boys again and having fun!

Achieving the goals that I had set out with this company, I decided to go back to school and gain another degree, this time in education. I had almost finished my studies when my husband's twenty-four-year employer decided to close its doors and we instinctively knew that we had to move from Ontario to British Columbia (BC). The timing could not have been more perfect, because the universe had other plans for my family and me. Once in BC, I still couldn't start teaching for the first year of our move. Apparently, transferring a degree from one province to another is not as easy as one would think.

I found part-time employment and volunteered at our three boys' school. I took extra time to assist my family in getting settled into our new province. I was also looking at adding to my résumé by starting my own business in intuitive consulting for men. Plus, I finally had found friends who thought similarly to me and shared some of my intuitive world.

WHAT THE HELL IS GOING ON?

What I noticed both in Ontario and in BC was there are so many places that women can go to explore, gather together, and study their intuition. You see, "we"—the women—usually refer to these as "Women's Circles." As I sat in these circles, I looked around the room and only ever noticed women. Even when the event was not advertised for "Women Only," there were never any men. I was surprised because we are all intuitive beings. Being a mother of three boys, having been surrounded by men my whole life, I thought, "What the hell is going on here? Why are men not here? Are they not interested in flexing their intuitive muscle?"

I discovered that you men are just as curious as or even more so than women. Yet, there was no way in hell you would sit in a "circle" and share your deep, inner feelings with women, let alone with other men, in this way. What I have found is that you process things internally (for the most part) while women do not. Men love to sit quietly in a reflective state while fishing, for instance. Women love to gather and openly discuss in a like-spirited community.

So there came about the idea of the title for this book as *Voodoo Shit for Men*. I decided to use this title entirely by accident in a conversation with my good friend, my publisher, Julie Salisbury. I was attending her Mastermind Workshop for inspiring authors. She has conjured up a phenomenal weekend during which the participants get a chance to work in collaboration by sharing ideas for their books. It is a very detailed, systematic curriculum and process that allows enthusiastic authors the opportunity to put together a methodical arrangement and plan for their books. Plus, it is filled with humour, fun, and exhilaration. On the second day of the workshop, it was my turn to discuss the main idea of my book, a short synopsis, and a few other details. I had considered two or three titles, and I was not committed to them at all. I was sharing a personal story with the participants and Julie about when I would discuss anything related to intuition, yoga, meditation, and so on with my husband and his response to me would always be, "Oh, you are talking about voodoo shit, right?"

Julie interrupted me in this precise moment and yelled out, "This is the title of your book—'Voodoo Shit,'" which I completed, "'For Men'!" We high-fived each other and laughed until our stomachs ached.

This book is intended to be fun (I hope) and light, if you will, to flex your intuitive muscle in your language. I must warn you: there may be an element of this book that might be a bit serious or Voodooish (yup, I just made up this word), due to the nature of what we are talking about. Intuition can be relatively subjective and not always backed up by concrete evidence to support it. Yet, rest assured, I will incorporate some type of humour, "Michèleism," joke to make you laugh, or a bit of swearing, when needed. I hope that I have succeeded thus far, because the opening was a bit serious; but it needed to be said or in this case written.

Basically, I want you to visualize (oops, a Voodoo word!); I want you to picture yourself sitting on a couch with me and we are talking as you read this book. I will share with you some of my experiences, my stories, my husband's story, and some of my clients' stories. You will gain some valuable insights into the workings of your own "spidey-senses," your gut instincts, your inner Voodoo Shit, your intuition, and how it "talks" to you every day. My hope is that you become more aware, more conscious of your surroundings, use your powers of observation to your advantage, and notice synchronicities (yikes, another Voodoo word), notice chance, luck, the causes and effects that occur on a daily basis, all of which will lead you in the correct, destined path.

Don't worry if you encounter a word that doesn't quite make total sense as I have included a glossary of definitions at the back of the book (thanks to a client suggestion). Most importantly, have fun, go with it, don't question it, and *for Peter's Sake*, get out of your head!

Okay, so, "Get out of your head!" What do I mean? I mean, stop thinking, give your pragmatic brain a rest, don't judge, don't question, don't doubt, don't rationalize, just don't! You can be very scientific and logical (at times). I want you to put all that aside for now. Yes, some of the information that I am going to present can be factual, as it has been studied and recorded, yet not all. You just need to trust and be willing to think outside the box. No, I did not screw that expression up. Good try!

Are you ready to have some fun? Let's get started!

My Husband Tim

"Train yourself to let go of everything you fear to lose."
Yoda

Tim is my husband of twenty-two years. We met at the ripe ages of eighteen and twenty. After dating for several years, we decided to get married. On the magical day of our wedding, I had a "feeling" that I would not be married to this man forever. I even recall telling my mother, "I can't do this." She informed me that I was simply nervous. Not wanting to have to explain this "feeling" I had to her, I continued marching down the aisle. I had never discussed with my mother how highly intuitive I really was. My intuitive abilities, my superpower continued to soar to new heights and I hadn't told my husband of this, my secret identity. I remained the silent observer, watching how he barely used his "spidey-senses," sometimes gently guiding him to listen more attentively, take more notice, and become more aware of his surroundings. Yet, he never knew the full extent of my true power.

Again, why did I not share this with him? Remember, I have never shared my secret identity with anyone up until recently.

As our lives unfolded together, I could sense that same "feeling" from over twenty years ago: "I will not be married to Tim forever." I did not feel that this would necessarily be a separation; rather I clearly sensed a death. Two things I confidently knew were Tim and I would not be married forever and Tim would die before the age of forty-five. It was "Till death do us part," literally.

I basically lived in fear each day of our marriage, dreading every hour he was late. I thought, "Is this the day he dies?" I hated sensing this. Knowing how intuition can be full of symbolism, I did further research with my gut. Asking for more clarity, I received similar messages based on my intuition of sensing Tim's death. I heard, I saw, I felt, and I knew Tim would die.

Ours was no different from most long-term relationships. We had our good times and our not-so-great times. I often initiated a conversation of my displeasure with our marriage. I used to get so pissed off when I witnessed Tim not following his intuition, his gut instincts. As I evolved over the years, I saw little or no intuitive changes in my husband. It made me so mad when he did something that would go against his gut. He wouldn't recognize that "feeling" even if it slapped him in the face. It wouldn't be until after a discussion that he'd mentioned having this "feeling" that something would go wrong, yet he continued on. Afterwards, he'd be surprised that the situation turned out crappily. I would simply shake my head. None of the subtleties that I hinted ever got noticed. *You can lead a cow to water, yet you cannot make her drink it*.

I wondered, "Why are we together if this man is remarkably blocked intuitively and not using his inner Voodoo power?" All the while, mine continued to intensify as the years passed. Ultimately, I reckoned this was my path and Tim was on his own journey. So I gave in and I revealed my secret identity. I told him almost everything, from what I saw, felt, sensed, and knew since I could recall. He did not quiver, get scared, doubt, or disbelieve me. He listened, deeply and attentively.

In the end, he asked, "Why did you never share this with me before?"

I could give no answer other than, "I have never told anyone else up until recently." I had only begun to share a bit when I attended a women's circle for intuition.

As a matter of fact, I hadn't even told my parents. As I think back over the years, my mother might have suspected my abilities by the books that adorned my shelves. One day she did mention to me how two of her brothers, my uncles, were also quite in tune with their superpower, their intuition. And, in my school days, there were friends who came to me regularly for "intuitive" advice.

Tim asked me again why I had never told anyone. My only response was that I didn't feel as though I needed to share knowledge of my superpower with anyone. He continued to probe and wondered if I ever felt scared or alone with everything I had experienced and continue to experience. I explained to him that I did not feel scared, ever. On the contrary, I always heard that I was protected and that my intuition, my gut instincts would lead me in the correct path. I had piqued his interest. He wanted to comprehend why he did not see the things that I saw, feel what I felt, or know what I knew. He asked me to let him know when I sensed something and to share it with him.

"What about everything else, like ghosts or spirits?" he asked.

Again, I explained that the spirits I saw were often relatives who had died and came to say hello, while the other group of spirits were people I did not know who had recently died and needed help figuring out what had just happened. Tim advised me to promise to tell him when I saw, heard, or felt a spirit in our house. And so, I do (for the most part).

I concentrated on building my business with my clients and sharing with my husband the insights from my clients' stories, while maintaining their privacy and confidentiality. This helped my husband get educated and I noticed that he flexed his intuitive muscle a bit more often. Even so, our marriage was slowly falling apart. We stopped communicating on a regular basis and we became distant. We were no longer on the same path, we argued more often and we were unhappy.

I sought out the advice of my closest friends and family members. When I voiced my thoughts of Tim's death, many would suggest that an emotional death would occur since our marriage was rocky. I would get so mad, because the signs that I kept receiving were indeed of a physical death.

Often, I'd find myself sitting alone, meditating, and asking for a clearer message. Over and over again, the feeling kept coming back—my inner Yoda voice said Tim's death would indeed be a physical death. My "inner Yoda voice" is one that is calm and collected, just as the Yoda character from *Star Wars* is himself. He is the Grand Master, the oldest and most powerful one who reminds us to let go of fear as it does not serve a purpose. I decided to try (optimal word) to let that thought go. It wasn't easy.

What I never did tell my husband was the fact that we would not be married forever because of his death. How does one tell their significant other, "By the way, you are scheduled to die before you are forty-five years old"? Consequently, I did not say that, and I suffered in silence with the knowledge of foreseeing his upcoming death.

Having children who are equally intuitive can be a detriment. I am positive they "picked up" on my vision of their father's death, as they would often joke with their dad. They'd say, "Dad, be careful to not do that or you'll die before you're forty-five years old."

Yes, we are the parents of three boys. Each of them has very special skills in the intuitive department and has been blessed to have a supportive mom such as myself. It is so important for me to teach my boys to respect, trust, and honour their intuitive muscles. There appear to be social parameters—a stigma—in today's society, if you will, which implies that intuition only belongs to women. I can authenticate this is not true. Although, there is nowhere for a man to flex, ignite, cultivate, and explore his intuitive muscle as freely as there is for women, this does not mean that you, the men, are not intuitive or that you do not want to learn more about it. You are flexing this muscle each and every day, yet you have not placed a label, a name to it, nor have you identified with the jargon. Hence this book, *Voodoo Shit for Men, Flex Your Intuitive Muscle.* I want my boys to know they are as much entitled to the right to use their intuition in guiding themselves through every path in their life as women are.

Allow me to introduce you to Ross, Maxwell (Max), and Théodore (T.J.).

Our Son Ross

"Ever since happiness heard your name, it has been running through the streets trying to find you."
Hafiz

Ross is a typical seventeen-year-old teenager, more or less. He is a good student who is about to graduate from high school and is highly motivated in achieving his goal of becoming a Heavy Duty Commercial Mechanic. Ross has jumped through many hoops to advance himself in striving to reach for his dream. Having been at his new high school for only three years, he chose to switch to a school that offered co-op courses in mechanics. Ross is a very social boy and found the second transition of changing schools much easier. He quickly made friends in his new setting while maintaining lasting friendships from his other high school. It is equally important for Ross to continue to pursue his French language studies and to graduate with a French diploma; therefore, he has been taking online French courses for the past two years. All the while, he continues to be physically active in the extreme sporting world of snowboarding and BMX racing. On top of that, let's add a girlfriend and a part-time job. He is a busy, devoted, and determined young man.

I knew Ross was especially intuitive from an early age, as most children are. I noticed, as a first-time mom, that my little boy would love to have stories read to him, yet rarely read them himself. He adored playing with blocks and would invariably choose to construct, design, or take apart toys and re-build them, rather than read a book. Ross had a wild imagination as a toddler and still does. When teachers in his younger grades strongly encouraged Ross to go to the reading centre instead of the building centre for playtime, he would obey; however, they often noticed he didn't read the stories; he just looked at the pictures. They were rightfully concerned that my little boy would not develop reading abilities, and thus, would miss out on the writing skills necessary to meet educational standards.

My husband and I learned much later on in his academic years that Ross is dyslexic. This diagnosis did not totally surprise us since we noticed Ross is more of a visual and artistic learner, basically meaning he learns more quickly and is able to retain more information and knowledge from charts, pictures, drawing, dioramas, building, and constructing. He needs to "see" things happening in his mind in order to remember and learn about them. This makes Ross very special. He can take apart an engine and place it back together almost without any assistance. He is exceptionally skilled and above average intelligence in the area of visual learning and the arts.

As a young child, Ross knew intuitively and naturally to go where he would excel. He did not want to disappoint himself by taking on a task he could not finish. His raw, authentic, gut instinct would guide him to the building blocks, the arts table, and the car station at the very young age of two. I recall sitting on the couch one day after school, asking my five-year-old Ross what he would like to do when he grew up. He answered without hesitation, "I want to work on big, big yellow trucks, Maman!"

His eyes sparkled so brightly as he proudly declared this statement. You see, Ross just always knew his superpower, his intuition, would guide him to make the right choices. He fullheartedly expresses to me that even when he races in BMX competitions, he follows his gut instinct during the race to either take a jump or not. Up to and including today, Ross has never suffered any major injuries in any extreme sports due to following his spidey-senses. He trusts them each and every time. He does not second-guess them and acts upon them in that instant.

While learning to drive a vehicle, Ross did the same thing. During a particular lesson, I asked him turn to left at the lights. The intersection was clear, yet he did not move ahead. Out of nowhere appeared a driver who would have hit us in the middle of our turn. My son explained that he just knew to not take the turn right away; he heard he needed to wait an extra minute. His intuitive muscle saved both our lives!

He learned quickly what happens when he does not follow his gut. When Ross was eleven years old, he was merrily playing with his neighbourhood friends. They decided to go jumping on the trampoline. The boys were having a splendid and jolly time jumping around. One of the friends suggested moving the trampoline closer to the tree and jumping off one of the branches. Can you "see" what will occur next? Is your intuitive tool of clairvoyance (a Voodoo word to be explained soon) working? Well, you guessed it… Ross thought it was a brilliant idea to be the first to take the plunge from the branch and land on the trampoline. He did not follow his intuition this time. As he jumped from the branch, he realized his mistake. Then, crashing into the trampoline, Ross broke his arm. A hard lesson to learn when you don't trust or take the time to reflect intuitively! He has learned to pay closer attention and be more aware of his gut instincts, thankfully!

There are many other intuitive tools and skills that Ross uses regularly. When people meet Ross, they often comment on how maturely he presents himself. They can see in his soulful eyes that he is wise beyond his years and possesses an old soul. In Ross's instance, this means he has a level of wisdom that most others his age do not have. His demeanour tells a story that he has lived many lives before. He is easy to get along with and knows when and how to be gracious. As for his values, ethics, and perceptions, Ross has quite high standards and often knows the difference between right and wrong immediately without being taught. This is an inherent trait of old souls. He also has a bigger picture view of the world and the Universe, and is very accepting of other people's beliefs.

Ross may or may not always trust, listen, or act upon his intuition every day of his life, although he is fortunate enough to have his brothers and me to talk to. He is quite comfortable and is very proud to inform me of times when he does indeed tune in with his superpower.

ॐ GRATITUDE JOURNAL

During the time I was raising Ross as a younger child, he taught me to appreciate and be thankful for the little gifts in life. I decided to start a gratitude journal as I was experiencing old discoveries through my little boy's eyes. A gratitude journal can take the form of pen and paper, a word document, a journal of your choice (yes, there are great choices for men, too), or a series of memos that you keep stored in your smart phone.

For your convenience, I have included in this book blank note pages that you can use as a journal to just jot down your thoughts. Please feel free to highlight words, phrases, and passages in this book, as well, and make notes throughout the margins and on the added journal pages when you feel compelled. Forget what your teachers taught you in school—to not write in your textbooks. As your personal intuitive trainer, I am giving you full permission to make as many notes as necessary while you read this book. Your intuition, your inner voice will speak to you when you least expect it; therefore, take a few minutes to record your intuitive hit as it occurs, so you can reread it later and see how accurate it is.

What does a gratitude journal do and how can it help improve your life? The basis of practising gratitude and writing down things you're grateful for, whether daily or a few times a week, is to bring awareness to the good encompassing our lives and to not take things for granted. Try recording the true gifts such as a new business deal, a new friendship, an unexpected surprise, perhaps your child's first words, mastering a new skill, or finding a five-dollar bill in your jean pocket. Sometimes, an entry can be that you are glad this crappy day is over and tomorrow will be a new day. I recommend writing in point form or making a short list of three to five items of thankfulness.

Robert Emmons, a professor at the University of California and the world's leading expert on the science of gratitude, instructs his participants in his research to "Be aware of your feelings and how you 'relish' and 'savour' this gift in your imagination. Take the time to be especially aware of the depth of your gratitude." He adds, "We tell them not to hurry through this exercise as if it were just another item on your to-do list. This way, gratitude journaling is really different from merely listing a bunch of pleasant things in one's life." Finally, Professor Emmons encourages us to form a habit of expressing gratitude for uplifting and inspirational events.

I found it took me twenty-one days to form this habit of writing down items of gratefulness. Once I established my habit, it became a day-to-day, moment-to-moment occurrence. When I receive a "gift" that truly encourages and creates positive emotions within me, I express a thank you, right then and there. Keeping a gratitude journal has also helped me through difficult and challenging times. We all have crap that we go through. With the help of a gratitude journal, the crap gets better more quickly. We all want to experience the best life possible filled with ultimate happiness, joy, and laughter. We would much rather be happy than not. Feelings of happiness and joy create less stress in our lives, help us to deal with negative situations with more finesse, and allow our intuitive muscle to be stronger. Try adding this easy-to-follow-and-use technique into your daily being and you will soon acquaint yourself with more positive feelings, moods, and emotions that are abundantly available for you.

Journal Notes

Our Son Maxwell

"The only thing worse than being blind is having sight but no vision."
Helen Keller

Our middle son Maxwell (Max) is fourteen years old and displays his raw, authentic intuitive muscle daily! He is not shy about getting in touch with his inner voice and he will often speak freely regarding this subject. You can find Max on my yoga mat sitting cross-legged in silence. True, at times, he is a clown and makes me laugh by pretending to be in an enlightened state of meditation, while on other occasions, Max will truly be quieting his mind. Usually this will occur when I least expect it, or, if we are on a tight schedule, Max will *walk to the beat of his own drummer*.

We have given Max a superhero name of the "Ultimate Butterfly Watcher." What do I mean by this? Picture if you will in your imagination, a boy BMX-racing with all his might on a dirt track. Without warning, Max stops his bike and runs off the track into the field. I wonder what has happened, thinking perhaps he has hurt himself. Suddenly, he reappears, gets back on his bike, and continues to race. At the finish line, I question my son as to why he decided to stop racing so abruptly. He smiles and answers that he spotted a hill of little green insects crawling about. Upon inspection, he discovered it was a praying mantis nest with little baby mantises covering the hill. Leave it to Max to appreciate such beauty in nature.

During the course of his fourteen years, this happens religiously. Max has finally learned to wait until after the BMX race is over before wandering off to inspect the latest miracle in nature. This is Maxwell's meditative and Zen-out state: he observes, he appreciates, and he is in the moment, especially when outdoors.

Maxwell is so attentive to his surroundings; he observes what most people do not even notice. He is quite conscientious, respectful, and adores Mother Nature. Beware if you are in a rush, as Max functions with his own rhythm and schedule. His response sounds a bit like the following when I try to rush him, "Mom, can't you see that I am busy at the moment…"

I also get the same response when he is "busy" being a couch potato. He joked one day when I asked him what he had planned for the day by replying, "I am striving to be a professional couch potato."

"Probably not the best intuitive choice of a career move," I joked back.

From a very young age, Maxwell has been attracted to the miracles he encounters. I found him at the age of two lying on the grass in deep concentration. As I approached him to find out what had captured his interest, I realized Maxwell was covered with ladybugs. He looked up at me, smiled, and I could tell he was in his ultimate glory. He continued to lie comfortably with ladybugs crawling on his hands, his back, and his arms. Maxwell informed me that each one is different despite looking the same at first sight. He lay in fascination for almost thirty minutes, quietly passionate from this discovery of beauty and awe.

Not only does Max notice the little things in life, he is also very empathetic to people around him. He can effortlessly lift the energy and the mood in a room by simply being present. Oddly, people will swarm to Maxwell, just as he does to insects and the animal kingdom. Perhaps, he should be called "Insect and Animal Whisperer," as he could tame a lion or a shark with his smile or his touch. His friends and his teachers regard him as the class clown who is always jovial, full of life, good natured, and lighthearted.

You may be wondering how this demonstrates Maxwell flexing his intuitive muscle. As I mentioned, he is able to quiet his mind chatter by getting in touch with nature and enjoying the simplicities of life. This allows him to focus better in school, have a positive outlook, be more attentive to details, and elevate his mood quickly. Being sensitive to other people's feelings, Maxwell is a good judge of character, exhibits compassion when needed, and is able to brighten the day as a lighthouse lights the way for boats at night. This intuitive quality will serve him well later on in life when making business transactions, knowing who to trust or not, and building relationships.

ॐ MEDITATION

You see meditation doesn't have to be sitting with your legs crossed in complete silence for hours on end on a Tibetan hillside, although that sounds delightful at times during our busy lives. Max has been able to teach me that a meditation can easily be incorporated routinely with everything we do in our lives, whether it is your favourite sporting activity, cooking, your hobby, walking, writing (just as I am doing today), or reading to your children, etcetera. What is important is to be completely involved and relaxed, to be in the present moment with yourself, the exercise at hand, and those with you. Let go of all other distractions from cellular phones to televisions, and just be in the moment to appreciate the time you are spending doing your treasured Zen activity with those you love. You will find your mind will quiet, your mood will lift, you will de-stress, you will feel more energized, and you'll have spent quality time with yourself and others. By viewing these actions as forms of meditation, you will find yourself sitting quietly concentrating on your breath flowing smoothly and your spidey-senses becoming more heightened and acute.

Meditation is a form of relaxation, a personal practice where you focus on a specific action such as breathing, or on a focal point; each time your mind wanders, you bring your focus back. Meditation is also when you bring your attention to your surroundings without reacting to them; you are simply observing or witnessing without attaching emotions to the events.

Some of the benefits of meditation are increased immunity; lower blood pressure; an overall sense of calmness; relieved physical tension and discomfort; increased focus, creativity, productivity, and memory; less anxiety and stress; regulated emotions; better sleep patterns; and so much more. The list is endless. Let's look at these in more detail.

IMMUNE SYSTEM

Meditation increases and boosts your immune system by relaxing your cells to produce a positive response to fight off diseases. In a study conducted by Harvard Medical School, Dr. Herbert Benson and his researchers discovered that practising relaxation in the form of meditation increased disease-fighting genes and fought inflammation, which is the cause of major diseases such as Alzheimer's, heart attack, and Crohn's Disease, to name a few. Dr. Benson noted in his research with participants doing regular meditative practice that their genes killed cells that were diseased and cancerous. Participants who regularly performed deep breathing, meditation, and relaxing exercises had less chance of developing arthritis and joint pain; certainly noteworthy information for all athletes. Athletes noticed that they experienced a decrease in overall injuries when they practised meditation and relaxation exercises. Furthermore, they had lower blood pressure and rarely got sick.

A study in 2008 under Dr. Randy Zusman showed that over 60 percent of patients with high blood pressure who meditated regularly for three months lowered their blood pressure. His studies explained that meditation forms nitric oxide, which opens the blood vessels. Moreover, we can see, through Dr. Herbert Benson's studies, that meditation can be beneficial to our physical bodies on cellular and molecular levels. Further research done through the University of California at Davis's Shamantha Project resulted in higher telomerase (the protective area of our chromosomes) activity, which is responsible for helping us live longer. The Ohio State University has conducted its own research on cancer patients who performed relaxation and meditation regularly, and noticed a reduction of cancer recurrences and tumours appearing in the elderly. Some other remarkable attributes meditation offers to your immune system are to decrease the severity of cold symptoms and lessen the chances of getting a cold or flu. Who doesn't want to be healthier?

LESS STRESS

"Stress" is everyone's favourite buzzword lately. Each of us is affected by stress on a constant basis, whether it is demands from work, demands from family, an illness, getting married, starting a new career, going to university for the first time, financial difficulties, being a perfectionist, negative self-talk, anxiety, a constant state of worry, being too busy, being pessimistic, celebrating the holidays, and so on. Stress is all around us (like Christmas) and it will never totally go away. It does not discriminate and affect only adults; stress is also part of the lives of young children, teenagers, young adults, and the elderly alike. Your social status, financial situation, marital status, gender, and educational level make no difference to stress. It'll affect each and every one of us, equally. What is important to realize is how to deal with stress, how to reduce stress in our lives, how to recognize the signs of stress as they are coming on, and how to minimize the effects of stress on our well-being.

Stress has many negative and destructive side effects on our bodies that cause diseases and illnesses. It afflicts not only our physical being; it also puts our emotional, spiritual (I don't mean "religious"), and energetic beings into a general state of disarray additionally. Yet, they are often ignored in the healing process when trying to deal with stress. Some of the symptoms of stress will present themselves as upset stomach causing digestive issues, muscle tightness and soreness causing injuries, headache causing lack of concentration, lack of sleep causing irritability, nervousness causing anxiety, impatience causing lack of self-control, and more. You will treat the symptoms by seeing a massage therapist to ease your achy muscles, taking an antacid to soothe your upset stomach, taking an aspirin for your headache, going to bed earlier, etcetera. These are all temporary fixes, Band-Aids if you will. You are not getting to the root of the cause: stress.

I have found that more of my male clients are stricken by stress than my female clients. You men are natural born protectors; hence, making your demands seems more stressful and it can induce a fight-or-flight response mentally. Add to that challenge having no outlets to reduce and eliminate the evils of stress on the emotional, spiritual, and energetic parts of your welfare, and the situation is clear. As I stated in an earlier chapter, women have so many avenues to explore their intuitive abilities: in circles, yoga classes, meditation workshops, and other types of gatherings; this, therefore, diminishes their stress and allows them to learn how to deal with stress on an energetic and spiritual level.

Are you stressed out yet?

There is good news, as meditation and deep relaxation methods help to release tension from your bodies (physical and energetic). Deep relaxation practices do not include lounging around watching your favourite television shows for hours on end or chilling out with a beer on the deck, despite the fact that that sounds quite appealing at times. Deep relaxation comes from receiving Reiki and hypnosis, going to a yoga class, doing some deep breathing, or exercising rhythmically. In a compelling article published by Active.com entitled "7 Ways Exercise Relieves Stress," Kelly Blackwin of Fitness Together in Santa Monica states that endorphins (the happy brain chemicals) are released during exercise, decreasing stress and depression. When you are in the flow of exercising, especially while running or cycling, your mind relaxes. Your sleep and rest are regular when you exercise, since you have established a positive pattern, which leads to a more productive day. The article suggests that when you are making a plan and setting goals for your workout, the skill of organization required to create the plan and the goals will filter into your daily life as well, and create a sense of achievement and accomplishment.

I suggest to my clients to practise whichever form of exercise best suits their stress level, and to vary it depending on stress, too. Also, selecting an exercise regime that you will actually do is highly important. No point committing to running a ten-kilometre marathon when you will not follow through. Choose an exercise that you enjoy and will do. The article states the same thing. Yoga and Pilates give you more energy; martial arts and boxing reduce anger and anxiety; and cycling, swimming, and running help you gain more control through rhythmic exercises. These are just a few suggestions for you to incorporate into your daily routine. I, for one, most enjoy yoga and Zumba—a dance fitness exercise routine to fun, upbeat music. My husband prefers exercising on the elliptical machine, while some of my clients do martial arts or play tennis as their exercise.

ॐ What is Reiki?

I mentioned that receiving Reiki is one way to go into deep

relaxation. It is also highly beneficial in reducing an overload of stress. Reiki is a natural, safe, ancient technique using healing, universal life force energy that flows through the Reiki practitioner's hands. Reiki is not connected to any religion, cult, dogma, or human belief system; therefore, all living creatures can enjoy its benefits. Reiki promotes healing; enhances relaxation; reduces stress and anxiety; heightens your intuition; calms mind chatter; clears toxins; balances the organs and body functions; strengthens the immune system; releases mental, emotional, physical, and spiritual blocks; and does so much more. It brings balance and harmony to the body, mind, and soul. It is important to realize that Reiki is a healing energy, not a curing energy.

I refer to Reiki as a massage for the energetic body. Whereas a massage therapist massages your physical body and muscles, as a Reiki Master-Teacher, I focus on your energetic body. Energy is all around us and is present in every living being, whether a plant, an animal, or a human. Even Hollywood has ventured into this field, and we see more sitcoms, television series, and movies dealing with Reiki. For example, *Grey's Anatomy* had an episode in which a Reiki practitioner gave a friend a treatment. Almost everyone has performed Reiki in one form or another in his or her lifetime without even knowing it. Think back to the last time you hurt yourself. What did you instinctively do? You placed your hands on your ache or pain to ease it and to heal it. Any parent does the same with their child when they get hurt too. We might say something to the effect of, "Oh, let Mama take the pain away...," or "Don't worry, the pain is all gone now. See, Daddy made it go away..." In those precious, instinctive moments, you were a Reiki practitioner and didn't even know it!

Reiki has a long history dating back to the 19th century; it was first developed by a Japanese priest and professor, Mikao Usui (1865-1926). His journey brought him to a twenty-one-day meditation and a fast on Mount Kurama where he became enlightened and received the answers he was seeking. He developed Reiki precepts and principles, because he strongly felt that an individual must take ownership of their healing and changing their lives. The age-old expression comes to mind: *"You can lead a cow to water, yet you cannot make her drink it."* The same is true of Reiki. A practitioner can perform Reiki on a client; yet, if that client doesn't change or evolve old habits, negative thinking, and negative patterns, then Reiki is not going to work to its full potential. The principles are easy to follow if you remember to live by them, one day at a time.

The Five Usui Reiki Precepts and Principles are:

- Just for today, do not anger.
- Just for today, do not worry.
- Just for today, honour your parents, teachers, and elders.
- Just for today, earn a living honestly.
- Just for today, give thanks to every living thing.

"Just for today" means in this moment in time. Forget about the past, as it no longer exists. Don't think about the future since it hasn't occurred yet.

I encounter so many clients who live in either or both the past and the future, and are full of worry, anxiety, fear, or anger. We can't physically change the past; we can learn from our experiences and use the lessons to move forward in the present moment. We can't live in the future either. We definitely can plan for a better future and get insights of what is to come. Try not to be too attached to specifics details, as they can at times prevent us from seeing the necessary happenings in this moment that could lead us to our destined future. So be here, right now, in this time.

If you are finding that situations are repeating themselves in your life, and are causing you to worry, be anxious, in a state of fear, or otherwise, then you must live through *Groundhog Day* all over again. Why? You have not learned what you were meant to, to move forward, to achieve the next steps, or to fulfill your dream, your goal. In the movie mentioned, the main character played by Bill Murray is an egocentric weatherman who repeats the same miserable and not-so-great day over and over. It isn't until he finally realizes that he must make significant positive changes in his life and his priorities that his day finally ends happily. Be the best man you can be with what you have in this moment in time. Listen to your gut and it'll not fail you.

The inscription on Mikao Usui's headstone reads, "If Reiki can be spread throughout the world, it will touch the human heart and the morals of society. It will be helpful for many people, not only healing disease, but the Earth as a whole."

I recommend to my clients to try visualizations, meditations, and Reiki during our sessions together, to diminish the effects of stress. I teach a simple meditation that my clients can do anywhere, anytime, on their own. A typical meditation that I like to do with my clients includes sitting comfortably, closing your eyes, focusing on your breathing, scanning your body, possibly using an affirmation or mantra, and incorporating imagery. With soft music playing in the background, my clients are often taken away to another world where stress doesn't exist, even for only a few minutes. I always advise them to not meditate while driving. Along with Reiki, other forms of natural healing such as hypnosis and acupuncture are very effective in maintaining a healthy lifestyle with less stress.

Focus, Creativity, and Productivity

Want more focus, creativity, and productivity? Then meditate, Zen out, and get your Reiki on! Our brain is an important organ that many of us ignore or take for granted.

There are four vital parts of the brain when it comes to meditation. They are the frontal lobe located at the front of the brain, which is responsible for emotions, judgments, empathy, reasoning, and self-consciousness; the parietal lobe located directly behind the frontal lobe relays the sense of touch and pain; the occipital lobe located at the back of the brain interprets visual stimuli; and the temporal lobe located toward the bottom of the brain relates the auditory responses and memory.

What actually happens in your brain when you are meditating is that more grey matter is produced, which slows down the aging process. Grey matter grows while you are meditating and, *like any other muscle when it is flexed*, the brain—the organ becomes stronger and more proficient. Neuroscientist Richard Davidson from the University of Wisconsin explains that higher levels of gamma waves and neuroplasticity are produced during meditation, causing the brain to evolve structurally and functionally. In essence, our brain is easily able to block out distractions and increase our productivity. Because the brain's cognitive ability improves, so does your memory, which can lead to better focus and therefore the increased productivity. Moreover, your body awareness, self-awareness, and attention to detail are increased through meditation; your chances for injury are drastically reduced; and your body's natural healing process is actively engaged. This means you can heal more quickly, which is especially beneficial for athletes, stunt performers, and people in careers where physical activity is required on a regular basis, such as police officers and fire fighters.

Creative ideas were sparked during a study conducted in the Netherlands at the Institute for Psychological Research and the Leiden Institute for Brain and Cognition. Participants were asked to undergo open-monitoring meditation (OM; no pun intended. When people meditate and focus on a mantra, they often choose the word "Om" to repeat; there will be more on this in the following paragraph.), in which participants' attention is flexible, they are open to perceiving without focusing on a specific item, and they are receptive to all thoughts and sensations.

Essentially, I am in an OM meditation right now, as I type through these words, simply allowing my thoughts to flow naturally. In essence, I am active in the process of typing, allowing the ideas to come to me freely without judging them or doubting them. I am simply the channel for the message. I notice which words or thoughts must be written or omitted as I type. I notice how my body is feeling. Are my legs falling numb from sitting too long in the same position? I am aware of surrounding noises from outside—the birds singing, my children laughing, the car driving by, and I simply hear them rather than pay attention and allow them to distract me. I do not stress that I will not finish the manuscript on time; rather I focus on what I need to do right now. I realize that my creativity is expanding as I glance to my previously written book notes, and that thought magnifies through the current state of writing.

You can do the same when you are active. You have an end goal in my mind, a strategy, and a plan. You notice cues and signals from your body—does your arm ache from the bruise, are you smiling and content while you are deeply involved in your task at hand? You become entranced in the activity and, all of a sudden, your creativity has increased through the act of OM meditation.

An example of this type of creativity I do with some of my clients to help them get in touch with their creative side is to take an object such as a plate. I ask them to think of what other object this plate could be. My client usually answers a steering wheel, a Frisbee, a hat, etcetera. Actors in drama school often do this same technique and exercise to help them expand their creativity.

Focused-attention (FA) meditation is when you focus on one

particular thought or object, as you would with a breathing exercise.

The researchers found that more creative thoughts and ideas came to those meditators who performed regular open-monitoring meditation because, as Sara Lazar, a leader of the study and a psychologist at Harvard Medical School states, "Our data suggest that meditation practice can promote cortical plasticity in adults in areas important for cognitive and emotional processing and well-being… These findings are consistent with other studies that demonstrated increased thickness of music areas in the brains of musicians, and visual and motor areas in the brains of jugglers. In other words, the structure of an adult brain can change in response to repeated practice."

The Om used in meditation is a Sanskrit word, a mantra, and a sound; its symbol is 🕉. It is a sacred symbol meaning "sound." Actually, the meaning of "Om" varies depending on what you read. I have been able to deduce that it means much more than any one source states. It is found in many Dharmic religions, such as Hinduism and Buddhism. Dharmic religions are those from Indian descent where "dharma" signifies a few different meaning from duties, laws, virtues, and the right way of living to cosmic law and order. Dharma is the basis of most Indian philosophies and religions. When "Om" is spoken in unison during a group meditation, it creates a drumming or humming sound that lifts the vibration, the energy of the participants. It is quite a powerful sound. Like most religions, Hinduism and Buddhism utilize a trinity of sorts, and the Om symbol seems to represent the trio, too. Om is the Universe and, in Hinduism, it is the three gods: Brahma, Vishnu, and Shiva who are equal to the heavens, the earth, and the underworld. It is believed to be a representation of the past, the present, and the future. Pretty much, Om is everything and anything that is, was, and will be. Try it someday in a meditation, and listen and sense how the syllable feels in your throat as you speak it.

I hope that I have been able to teach you a bit more as to why meditation—no matter the form of this relaxation practice you use—is so vital in maintaining a healthy lifestyle and a balanced physical, emotional, and energetic whole you. So get your Om on!

Journal Notes

Our Son Théodore

"The only real valuable thing is intuition."
Albert Einstein

Our youngest son, Théodore (T.J.) is eleven years old and has been actively engaged with his superpower from a young age as well.

Most children are very in tune with their instincts, until of course they grow up or out of them. As they become teenagers, they are pressured into participating in activities that go against their will, but they do them anyway. (This even happens to us as adults.) Or, they begin to question what they hear, see, or feel and, if their parents or the other adults in their lives do not have the answers, the child begins to doubt what they are encountering with their superpower. So in the end, it fades away and it becomes more difficult to flex your intuitive muscle as an adult, especially if you are a man.

This is where I come in as I mentioned before. I believe it is equally critical for a man to be in touch with his intuition as it is for a woman. Remember, intuition doesn't only belong to women! This is why I have been blessed with three boys—to learn the ins and outs of what it means to be a man (or as best I can). As I stated earlier, you men do not seem to have the same access to workshops to explore your intuition, your own superpower. For the most part, the few workshops that I have attended have either advertised "Only for Women" or only women show up. No more, I say! So this book, *Voodoo Shit for Men*, is for you. It's the Boys Only Club of Flexing Your Intuitive Muscle with your Personal Intuitive Trainer, me!

Getting back to T.J., I noticed that he has not yet questioned his spidey-senses; rather he has been very accepting of them. I recognized—remembering my younger years—similarities to what he is undergoing. I decided to sit with my son one evening and question him. He was open, honest, and expressed some concern as to why certain things were happening to him. T.J.'s strongest spidey-senses are seeing and feeling. He is a very sensitive individual who will easily pick up other people's feelings and notice their emotional states. He will automatically know if someone is kind, upset, in a good mood, or not. He will trust and gravitate toward individuals who are sensitive and intuitive like himself. People have often told me they see a deeper knowing in T.J.'s eyes, despite having just met him. For example, T.J. arrived home from school with his brothers one day when I was finishing up a client session. As always, I introduce my children to my clients, and in this case, T.J. walked over to my client and asked if he could give him a hug. My client looked at me then to T.J. and agreed. My client was impressed how my son was able to pick up that he needed a hug in that moment. Having such acute superpowers has helped T.J. assess situations and act accordingly. Despite having an inquisitive mind and questioning everything around him, T.J. displays greater acceptance and understanding.

Much like Ross, his oldest brother, Théodore has known what he wants to do as a career from a young age. T.J. could literally sing and dance before he talked and walked. If you were to ask him today what he'd like to do when he grows up, he will often respond, "Be the next Justin Bieber." The Bieber prior to the huge mess he is in now.

T.J.'s teachers occasionally misunderstand him, as he is an active little boy who loves to move around. For him, learning comes effortlessly through movement and rhythm. His creative juices flow smoothly when he is able to stand up, move around, sing out loud, or dance about. Every morning and night, we hear Théodore sing when he awakes and sing when he falls asleep. Jumping out of bed in the morning, he rushes upstairs to say a cheerful, "Good morning," followed by a dance. This annoys his brothers most mornings, yet T.J. doesn't seem to be bothered by their reactions as he continues to allow his raw instincts to guide him.

ॐ MEDIUMSHIP

Like his two brothers, T.J. will see, hear, and feel spirits and ghosts that others do not notice. This is referred to as "mediumship." Mediumship is the ability to communicate with the dead—with ghosts who are stuck on the earth plane and also with spirits of loved ones who have passed away. The purpose of this book, *Voodoo Shit for Men,* is not to educate you on the ins and outs of mediumship, yet I do think it necessary to speak of it, just in case you are one who has had dealings with the afterlife and the spirit world. If not, you can skip this interesting topic and move on. Or, if you are naturally curious and you are an out-of-the-box thinker, I would love you to read on.

One of the biggest misconceptions about ghosts and spirits is that they are here to harm, scare, or terrify human beings. They are not. Typically, they have unfinished business with their surviving relatives and want a message to be delivered to them. There are countless other reasons why spirits and ghosts choose to communicate with the living. The spirit will seek out a living human being who is susceptible and open to their reality, and perhaps willing to decipher what they are trying to say. Mediumship has been practised for centuries and will continue to be. It is always a good idea to interview a medium—like me—who can be very helpful and genuine in helping you communicate with your loved ones in the other realms. I always recommend to my clients when they are seeking out a medium to have in mind a specific relative who has passed away. Interview the medium to investigate whether they are able to pick up on a certain quality, character trait, favourite colour, odour, hobby, etcetera of your deceased relative. The process of interviewing and checking testimonials or references will validate a medium's credibility, even if that medium is me.

Mediumship is not based on intuition, per se, although some of the same tools and skills demonstrated in seeing and hearing ghosts are employed. The avenue of mediumship is not for everyone, as many people are apprehensive and a bit fearful of venturing down this road. I decided to write briefly about this topic in case you have recently seen a spirit or a ghost. Please note that, as a parent, if you have children who have "imaginary friends," I am willing to bet these "friends" are spirits or ghosts. Maybe, you even had "imaginary friends" as a child yourself. I did. This does not mean they or you are socially inept; rather, it means they are connecting to something greater and magical. The next time your child seems to be talking to someone you can't see, ask them what is happening and believe them.

One of my clients shared with me this story about one of his twin daughters. He and this twin were driving to their family summer home to join his wife and the other twin who were already enjoying their first few days of vacation. The twin daughters were eight years old. My client's mother had passed away while his wife was pregnant with the girls; therefore, they had never met their grandmother. Driving along the stretch of the highway in beautiful British Columbia can be treacherous due to the mountains and the wildlife. Father and daughter were enjoying their one-on-one time together, chatting about what they would be doing for the next couple of weeks, when his daughter interrupted him and said, "Grandma Jane wants you to slow down, because up ahead there is a family of deer crossing the highway, Daddy."

He was puzzled by this comment and looked in the rearview mirror to see his daughter conversing with his mother in the back seat of the car. He confessed to me that, for only a split second, he had seen his mother; she had disappeared as quickly as he had seen her. He remarked that his daughter continued to have a lovely conversation with her grandmother for approximately one to two minutes. As he slowed down in the bend of the highway based on the advice of his deceased mother, he saw the family of deer crossing the highway. From that moment on, he never doubted the abilities of his daughters to relay messages to him from his mother. He said to me in closing, it was as though his mom knew her granddaughters would not question her spirit and would say what she asked of them.

Please remember, as I said, children are very sensitive. They are prone to communicating with spirits and ghosts, are highly intuitive, and act on raw, organic instincts, as do animals.

Animals inherit their instincts from their parents, and their raw gut instincts are engrained early on. This explains how baby birds know how to get food from their mothers and bears know to hibernate in the winter months in order to survive. Without their engrained instincts, many animals would not survive and would probably perish and become extinct through natural causes. The opposite is true, as many animals continue to thrive and adapt to their ever-changing habitats by following their natural instincts.

Children are no different. They are instinctive and act on their instincts all the time. When a baby is hungry, he or she will cry. The same baby will cry out for a diaper change, if he or she is too hot or cold, or wants attention, and so forth. If you pay close attention as the parent of this baby, you will notice each cry is a bit different depending on what your baby needs. As the baby grows into a toddler, we—the adults—describe this stage of our precious child's life as the "terrible twos." I want you to shift your thinking away from the old-school "terrible twos" to the new-age discovery stage of the two-year-old. Aged two, your child is discovering the world for the first time on his or her own. They are much more mobile, have no boundaries, and want to try everything for themselves. Their instincts will guide them through emotional outbursts, since they do not have the maturity to vocalize their frustrations or wants as adults do. They are struggling between wanting to be more independent and clinging to your leg. As the two-year-old becomes three, they will expand their vocabulary and may be able to communicate their emotional state and wants more efficiently. They are still learning new things each day, gaining their independence, and again their natural instincts guide them.

Back to mediumship. You may or may not want to refine your skills and abilities to be able to talk to the dead. This is your choice. I simply want to put it out there so you know it exists and can very well manifest in your reality anytime, especially if you are flexing your intuitive muscle. But then again it may not. It entirely depends on you. If you are interested in cultivating and learning more about mediumship, please be sure to connect with me.

T.J. has such vivid dreams that he will wake up in a scare shouting for me in the middle of the night, especially if he has had visitors throughout his sleep. I have asked him if he recognizes the spirits. He answers he does not. He is uncertain if he is completely afraid or not. I suggested he try to communicate with the spirit or ghost and find out more information. I prompted him to ask questions such as, "What do you want? Why are you here to see me? What do you have to say? Do you want me to do something for you?"

T.J. asked me why he should do that. Sincerely, I suggested he see if he can help the spirit, as perhaps they are lost, lonely, afraid, and unsure of what is happening to them. Or maybe, they want to chat.

Without missing a beat, T.J. inquired if there are greater, lighter beings such as angels who can assist and protect him while he sleeps. He admitted that some nights it is difficult to get a full night's sleep as too many spirits and ghosts are roaming around talking to him or watching him in his room. I suggested he ask his great-uncle who has passed away to protect him during his rest. He was fine with summoning his great-uncle's spirit, although T.J. demanded a name of an angel he can call upon for "ultimate protection." I gave him a few names such as Archangel Michael and Archangel Raphael.

Since our talk that evening, T.J. has not woken up screaming in the middle of night. However, he does continue to have visitors while he sleeps, yet they do not scare him any longer. Instead, he tells me he is helping them find their way home. I know this sounds a bit "supernatural," yet I assure you in my home this is no big deal; it is a typical occurrence to encounter a ghost or two.

We moved last summer to a different house. We wanted a house with a bigger yard and more open space. When I shared with some friends the house we decided upon, a few commented, "Isn't that the haunted house?" I laughed and replied, "No, it isn't haunted, but there is a friendly, resident ghost." They looked at me confused and persisted in stating that if a ghost lives in your house, then your house is haunted. I beg to differ, as the ghost in our house is not trying to scare us; he simply likes being here and does not bother us. Have you ever seen an episode of *Ghost Whisperer*, *Angel*, or *Supernatural*? Well, welcome to my world.

Some of T.J.'s other dreams are premonitions to events that will occur in the near future in his life or in the lives of other people he knows. T.J. will often discuss these with me and rather than tell him they are not real, they are "just" dreams, or to forget about them, we analyze them together. We search for meanings, messages, and answers in the dreams that will assist him in decision-making for future events. Through his dreams, T.J. is gathering information intuitively that will serve a purpose for a later date. This will create a sense of déjà-vu in his life and subsequently my life as his mother.

We can all relate to déjà-vu; its function in a sleep state is to prepare us for future events that have not entered our consciousness yet, through our daily life. Typically, this can happen to forewarn us about traumatic events such as car accidents or trouble ahead. It allows us to make different choices as we recognize the situation from the dream we already had. This creates a sense of empowerment as we allow ourselves to foresee our future, even if through a dream state. Perhaps you have dreamed of placing your house on the real estate market just before the market slows down, or of applying for a different job just before your employer decides to close its doors and go out of business. There will be subtleties throughout your existence that will lead you to remember a premonition—a déjà-vu—so you can react accordingly.

ॐ SYNCHRONICITIES

Synchronicities will probably be a big part of your life too. The online *Merriam-Webster Dictionary* defines the word "synchronicity" as "the coincidental occurrence of events and especially psychic events (as similar thoughts in widely separated persons or a mental image of an unexpected event before it happens) that seem related but are not explained by conventional mechanisms of causality—used especially in the psychology of C. G. Jung" (www.merriam-webster.com). In their book, *The 7 Secrets of Synchronicity*, Trish MacGregor and Rob MacGregor define synchronicity as "The coming together of inner and outer events in a way that can't be explained by cause and effect and that is meaningful to the observer" (Adam Media, Avon, Massachusetts).

In other words, synchronicity is when you notice something happening in your life right now that may appear to be a coincidence at first glance, until it occurs again or in a very similar fashion, usually very close together in time to the first occurrence.

For instance, a client of mine had felt a presence around for a few days. As he was unclear as to who the presence was, I suggested that he ask its identity the next time he felt it. He thought it strange to speak to a presence he could only feel and not see; yet he gave it a try. A few days later, he called to inform me that the presence was his dad who had been dead for almost five years. I inquired how he knew for certain it was so. He explained that a series of synchronicities had led him to believe this presence to be his dad, one-hundred percent. He already knew what synchronicities were as we had finished a session on examining them and how they guide us.

One vital point I did mention to him was to pay attention to whether the synchronicities occurred three in a row. I cautioned him to realize "in a row" didn't mean precisely all at the same time, rather one synchronicity today, one tomorrow afternoon, and one in the evening. Or, something to this effect. He hesitated at first to believe that what he felt was his dad, because he was a skeptical man. He heard my words advising him to trust what he felt immediately, to not question the feeling, and just to get out of his head. Following my advice, he did that; then the synchronicities came full force. The same day he felt the presence and asked who it was, he was flipping through old family photographs for his son's collage project for a family tree. He indicated the only photographs in this particular box were entirely of his dad, despite the label reading "family photos." The next day searching through the garage for a tool, a chair fell off the hanger, which (you guessed it) belonged to his dad. That same evening, he felt the presence again. He decided to greet the presence with a resounding, "Hey, Dad!" Following the greeting, he gasped as the photograph of his dad on the fireplace mantel fell over. He concluded that this presence he had felt for the last few days was indeed his dad. He confessed to me that he would never again doubt his inner Voodoo Shit. This is another example of how mediumship and intuition are related.

ॐ Dream Journal

T.J.'s dreams are as realistic as my childhood and adult dreams. That awareness led me to create a dream journal, much like the gratitude journal I spoke of earlier in this book. I had more or less been recording some of my dreams from time to time. When I wanted to remember the specific details of a particular dream, it seemed as though it started to fade away. A dream journal can be old-fashioned pen and paper, a word document, or even a memo on your favourite electronic gadget. Again, please feel free to use the inserted pages in this section for your dream journal; therefore, it'll be easy for you to refer to them later on.

The purpose of the dream journal is to document all dreams that are vivid, appear real, memorable—good or bad, or those you feel compelled to write about. I recommend you keep the journal close to your bed, as it is either in the middle of the night or very early in the morning when you remember your dream. Typically, after about an hour of being awake, starting your morning routine, you'll most likely have forgotten your dream. So do try to record it immediately or shortly after you wake up. If you do not recall every detail, don't sweat it. Simply write about what comes naturally to your memory.

Once you have written out your dreams, I propose you keep them and reread them periodically to see if there is any significance between them and your waking life. It might be that the dream has hidden messages or answers to questions you are wondering about. Never discount a dream for being "just" a dream, especially if the details are poignant and engrained in your memory.

Also, you need to pay greater attention to recurring dreams as they are guaranteed to serve a powerful purpose. Whether it is a nightly, weekly, monthly, or annually recurring dream,

I strongly advise you to be attentive when it occurs. If the nature of the dream is nightmarish, pay even closer attention, as your subconscious mind is trying to bring the message to the surface. If the dream is not so much a nightmare, yet you continue to dream it, again be conscientious about recording the details that resurface in the many dreams. The essence of the dream is the same: it's a message for you. These dreams often occur during times of transition, if you have a problem to solve, a disagreement left unresolved, a situation where more clarity is required; or the focus may be a personal character trait that needs adjusting. Until you find your answer, the recurring dream persists, like a movie—even a bad movie—replaying over and over.

I look back occasionally on dreams I have recorded in my journal—both recurring and single—and still find value in them today, depending on what is happening in my life. I may consider rereading a past dream more times than once, as it still might play an integral part in giving me guidance and support in an on-going issue. All of my clients who have integrated this practice of recording their dreams find it an easy, useful, and meaningful exercise that provides them with an extra tool in their box of intuition tips.

Journal Notes

Your Toolbox

"Always pass on what you have learned."
Yoda

Your Spidey-Senses, Your Gut Instincts, Your Inner Voodoo, Your Intuition

What is intuition? "Intuition" as defined by the *Merriam-Webster Online Dictionary* is "A natural ability or power that makes it possible to know something without any proof or evidence; a feeling that guides a person to act a certain way without fully understanding why; something that is known or understood without proof or evidence." *The Collins Canadian English Dictionary* defines intuition as "Instinctive knowledge or insight without conscious reasoning." My definition for intuition is "The power of knowing without reason or intellect by being connected to your higher self—your gut instincts—your spidey-senses—your inner Voodoo voice." Intuition can be a hunch, a feeling, and a foresight. You will often hear women refer to their intuition as their "mother instinct."

From your perspective, intuition is your gut instinct, your spidey-sense, your inner Voodoo Shit, and the "feeling" that you know you are right. I am certain you have all experienced this at least once in your lifetime.

Here's one major difference between a man's intuition and a woman's intuition. You men don't always need to share absolutely every reflection. You are happy sitting silently fishing with your buddies while contemplating life in general. Women, on the other hand, feel a need to discuss with other women how their intuition works; hence, the reason for women's circles of intuition. Not that there is anything wrong with this. I see great value in gathering together discussing like-hearted subjects. Great minds think alike, just as great hearts feel alike. And women have huge hearts. Then again, so do men. Women need to seek confirmation that their intuition is correct and guiding them along the right path. Women will gather with friends and have a circle to discuss intuitive guidance. Men will accept intuition as raw material, an instinctive knowing, and move on. As with most of my clients, you may not even realize it is your very own superpower, your gut instinct, and your intuition at play. There is no need to discuss what you "think" might be intuitive guidance, until ... "In hindsight, I should have ..." You can hear it now, can't you? In this book, I will give you tips and tools to avoid those dreaded words of, *"In hindsight, I should have, I could have…"*

MY INTUITION

I have been blessed and at times cursed with this amazing innate gift of a highly active and accurate intuitive muscle my whole life. I can see into the past, present, and future of my life and of others'. I have chills down my spine when I encounter a déjà-vu moment. I experience things that others do not. I can also see, feel, hear, and sense what most people don't even believe exists, and only see in movies. For lack of a better word, I have been called a "psychic." I refer to myself as a highly intuitive personal trainer, since I mentor and counsel my clients on learning more about their own intuition, their gut instincts.

As a young child, I never once questioned what was happening to me. I simply trusted and, most importantly, I never knew any differently. I can sense when people around me are happy or sad. I can tell when the energy in a room is off or if something has happened there, especially bad things, like a fire or a murder. I can see colours projecting from all living creatures and beings, including plants. A memory comes to mind of when I was around the age of seven and I asked my mother, "Why are the people in church glowing?" I was seeing the people's auras.

When a friend is troubled and confused, they come to see me and ask for advice, only later to come back cheerfully proclaiming, "Michèle, you were right. How did you know that I needed to…?"

I also had and continue to have tingles and electrical sensations radiating from my hands every time I would hurt myself and without thinking, I would place my hands on the injured part of my body. I would feel instant relief. If I am unsure of what my next action step is, I sit quietly and the answer just appears.

A friend recently said to me in conversation that when my "psychic" gifts came into play he thought about "those" people who were weird and he had difficulty grasping the whole concept; however, he stated I was the most "normal" person he's ever met who has this unexplainable gift. Most importantly, he stated that we are good friends.

Did I think that others around me were having the same "feelings"? I don't think I did. At no time did I ask any of my family members and friends if they too had these "feelings" or visions. Not once, did I discuss with anyone, not even my parents, what I was experiencing or seeing. Reflecting back as to why I didn't share my gift with anyone else, I realize it was probably for fear of being judged as different, not fitting in, or being too weird. Well, I guess it is too late for that, since I have just written all about it.

I have since discovered that this gift is shared by some of my relatives on both sides of the family, from uncles to grandparents and cousins. What I know for certain is my gift has always remained with me and grown stronger as the years have passed. Over time, I have been able to identify my experiences and label them with words. Prior to that, I didn't even know the jargon or the terms. "Intuition." What was that? This word did not enter my vocabulary until much later in my life.

At around the age of thirty-five, I did ask my mother if she remembered anything special or different about me as a child. She responded that, when I was a baby in my crib, I would laugh, talk, and look at something in the corner of my room so intensely (something that she could not see), that she truly believed I was conversing with someone there. I went on to briefly explain to my mother some of the experiences that I had had up until then. Before that day, I had kept all this to myself. I could share so many stories, yet I shall save them for another book.

Your Inner Voodoo Shit

I do not claim to be an expert in the arena of intuition, only very competent and sophisticated. Intuition can be complicated, misunderstood, and misread. There exist so many variables, symbols, circumstances, perceptions, and choices that can easily change the outcome. I do not believe that anyone can claim to be an expert. My goal with this book is to show you that your own superpower, your intuition, your gut instincts are present every day, and they guide you in the choices you make—right or wrong.

Even your own intuition has always been present; granted it may be rusty and need some TLC to get it back in shape. Think of this book as your personal intuitive toolbox.

What does your inner Voodoo Shit look like? There are many different forms of intuition. I will list some of the basic tools to begin with, explain them, and provide some practical exercises for you to use in your daily life, both for business and personal use. You will have a good start of tips and tools to fill your toolbox so you can make laser-focused decisions, access your gut instincts in highly charged scenarios, and utilize your inner force to attract and manifest what you deserve and want out of life. Additionally, your powers of observation will increase, become laser-focused and fine-tuned. Your creativity, productivity, and calibre of expertise will elevate to new heights. You will be able to cultivate patience to allow your next business deal to flourish when the time is right. Your concentration, your overall performance and stamina will strengthen. You will transform negative self-talk into positive reinforcement, plus you will learn to quiet your mind chatter.

So grab your Superman cape, your *Star Wars Lifesaver*, your Lightsabre, your Batmobile, rev up your engines, and get ready for the ride of your life.

How Many Clairs are There?

For the most part, men need and love their tools. You have sheds, toolboxes, tool belts, a workbench, and most importantly, a garage full of tools. You have hammers, nails, saws, wrenches, and screws, funky starred, square, and flat screwdrivers (I don't profess to know these by their "official names"), and more. Each of these items has a specific purpose of its own and can be used in conjunction with another.

You use tools to fix, repair, build, and construct objects. There is no difference between your physical tools and your tools of intuition that assist you during the day. You can use intuition to course-correct an action, ask a question, gain clarity, and gather information. You can flex your intuitive muscle many ways, so let's count the ways.

I will start with the "Clairs" of your spidey-senses. "Clair" is a French word meaning "clear." There are four major clairs you'll want to attach to your tool belt. As with any tool, you may not use it every day, while at other times, you'll need to use many all at once, depending on the project at hand. My hope is for you to become familiar enough with each tool that you can pull the right one out at a moment's notice or use them in conjunction with one another.

It will be essential for you to get to know each tool and try the exercises that I suggest. There are many more exercises I could have included in the book; however, with the assistance of some of my clients, I chose the easiest to follow out of their favourites. Please try each tool on for size, as they are all so very useful. You might want to alter, change, or personalize the exercises a bit for your betterment. Once you have gained confidence with one tool, move on to the next. For the ease of understanding and full appreciation of each clair, try one exercise at a time until you are comfortable with how it works for you. As a result of practising and getting to learn the tools individually, you will find you have a favourite tool that you use more often and then rely on another one as backup or confirmation of the intuitive knowledge you have received. Only you will decipher which clair you prefer and feel most comfortable with.

Ready?

Get your tool belt on!

Clairvoyance—Do You See That?

"What makes Superman a hero is not that he has the power, but that he has the wisdom and the maturity to use the power wisely."
Christopher Reeve

Your first tool in the clair department is "clairvoyance," which is the ability to see clearly, using your third eye. The online dictionary defines "clairvoyance" as "the supernatural power of seeing objects or actions removed in space or time from natural viewing" (www.dictionary.com).

Traditionally speaking, clairvoyance allows your eyes to pick up and see things in an extrasensory way that relays intuitive meaning to your life. There are various types of screwdrivers, and the clairvoyant tool comes in many sorts; however, for the purpose of this book, I have chosen to explain only how it relates to the intuition that guides you. Many of you may find you see "other things" that are not related to your intuition, as my sons and I do.

Your clairvoyance can appear in moving colours, shapes, lifelike images, or in black and white. It can appear as a still image or a movie running through your mind's eye. You may see visions during a meditation; your clairvoyance is activating. Or, you might be able to recall each detail of a dream, thinking that it felt real. This too can be related to your clairvoyant tool.

Earlier on I suggested that you keep a pen and paper (or this book) near your bed so you can write down your recurring or vivid dreams, as this is your intuitive muscle of clairvoyance flexing. Imagine that you have eyes all around your head. My mother used to tell my siblings and me that she had eyes behind her head, as she always knew what we were doing.

If you are noticing a particular number, symbol, animal, or object reappearing in the course of your day, or over a short period of time, your clairvoyance is active. Pay attention, boys, and *smell the tea*. One very important piece of advice is to not judge what you are seeing. Do not question it, do not second-guess it, and do not discount it. Go with your initial thought, as this is how your intuition works. Your intuition strikes first, then your ego, then your brain, and your rationalizations come afterwards. Have fun while flexing your clairvoyant muscle. You have X-ray vision just like Superman, and you can do anything, just like the rock band R.E.M. says.

ॐ CLAIRVOYANCE EXERCISE

Lie in a comfortable and relaxed position on a blanket in the grass or the beach on a day when the sky is blue and filled with big, white, fluffy clouds. With your eyes half open, simply observe the clouds. What shapes, images, objects, symbols, letters, numbers appear in the clouds? You can record what you see in the clouds on your iPad, on a piece of paper, in this book, or take a picture of it.

"See" if there is a deeper meaning to what you see in the clouds. Does what you see have relevance to what is happening in your life right now? Gather information from what you observed in the clouds without judging it and simply be the eyewitness. Remember at the beginning of the book, I asked you to "Get out of your head"? This is when you'll need to take this advice to heart. Rather than question, doubt, fear, rationalize, and discount what you see in this exercise, simply accept it, trust it, and go with it.

Over a period of time, you will begin to observe and see

many "hints" around you that answer your burning questions and give you more insight to guide you smoothly through your life. Let your powers of observation be some of your greatest and most trusted tools.

CLIENT STORY #1—OFF TO THE RACES ... WITH A BMW M5. WHAT?

Mandeep is a successful real estate lawyer and has been one of my clients since the very conception of my personal intuitive training business of Spiritual Ventures. We met at a Real Estate Networking group two years ago where I gave him a complimentary Intuitive-Reiki session and he has been hooked ever since.

At that time, Mandeep was struggling to let go of his past and move forward. He described himself as an impatient man who felt much like a pressure cooker about to explode. Mandeep knew little about his intuition, did not meditate, and enjoyed sports, motorcycles, and time with his children. He also stated he felt damaged by women and didn't trust them. His reasons for seeking out my services were to help him get in touch with himself and to make laser-focused decisions to improve his business.

I recall asking Mandeep, during our initial meeting, why he trusted me since in the past he hadn't trusted women. He responded by saying that our relationship felt different; it was strictly about his emotional well-being and I would help him gain knowledge about himself, his superpower, his instincts. I felt truly honoured that he could trust me with his precious feelings that were obviously still hurting. Besides, my services are all about him, I explained. My work is to help him heal those feelings and be the best man he can be to himself and then to others.

I gave Mandeep many exercises to ignite his inner Voodoo

and to heal his past, which he did (most of the time). He noticed a huge improvement with many of his relationships with women. Mandeep also found the exercises quite easy to incorporate into his daily life and at the office. He took a few moments each day to practise his newfound skills and he amazed himself regularly. He was impressed with how simple each tool was to add to his tool belt and form into a habit. Each new development I witnessed in his intuition—a sign that his superpower was getting stronger—I acknowledged and applauded him. He began to feel much better.

One of his dreams was to own a BMW M5. Mandeep was currently driving (in my opinion) a pretty, hot looking BMW; yet the one he wanted was very expensive and he was not in a financial position to buy it. I suggested that he manifest the car through some visualization exercises, which he followed. He placed a picture of the BMW M5 as his screen saver so he could see it every day.

This is creating a vision board—if you will—placing images of items from different categories in your life that you want to come true. It is a form of starting with an intention, setting a goal, and taking the action steps to make it happen. The items may include material goods such as a new house, a new set of golf clubs; they may be lifestyle choices such as healthier eating, adding more vegetables to your food, new relationships whether they be business or personal, a reward for yourself in the form of a vacation, educational goals such as going back to school, personal advancement through your own research, and reading this book.

Life was good for Mandeep and he decided to take a break from my services during the Christmas holidays. The next time I saw Mandeep in the New Year, he was driving his dream car! He explained how working with me was an integral part of his life, in which he was able to manifest the most amazing and lucrative client who gifted him his dream car, his very own

BMW M5! It was the happiest, proudest moment in his life and he beamed as he drove us to the park for our session.

Sitting at the table, Mandeep and I discussed what his new goals were for the year. Business was good, life with his children was wonderful, and he was leaning toward a career transition. What he wanted to know was when he would no longer practise law, when he would gain his health back, since he had gained a bit of weight over the last few months, and when business would be more financially stable.

I questioned him. "I thought business was good; besides you are driving your dream car."

Apparently, he hadn't made another deal quite as fruitful as the last one and business was suffering. So back to the drawing board we went.

Mandeep's favourite tool is clairvoyance. I often employ this one during his sessions and get him back in touch with it. The table where we sat in the park was littered with rocks and a newspaper; we had not put them there ourselves. We began focusing on his question of when he should transition careers. I intuitively saw the numbers one and three. I asked Mandeep what he saw. He sat silently, as he continued to stare at the rocks in front of us. I too noticed the rocks. I typically try to give the client some time before I offer my intuition. I want their intuitive muscle flexing, giving them an answer that I can confirm with my initial intuitive hit.

With deep concentration, Mandeep asked me why I thought the rocks were there. I answered him with the following question, "Don't you think they are an answer to when your career should transition?"

He persisted in wanting to know what my spidey-senses were seeing for a timeframe. I decided to tell him. I replied with what I saw.

It is a challenge to place absolute knowing with timeframes, since many factors are involved, including free choice.

Quizzically, he counted the rocks. There were thirteen (13) rocks. His eyes started to glimmer with hope and he laughed. The wind started to pick up and Mandeep noticed the newspaper had flown open to page number thirteen. He laughed again. I looked over to his new car and counted the three numbers on his licence plate; they totalled thirteen. We laughed together, this time.

In the course of the next few days, he continued to see those two numbers in his surroundings: in his phone, on the clock, in telephone numbers, and even on my licence plate. Meanwhile, he asked if the two numbers meant one to three years or thirteen months. I reminded him that thirteen months is more than one year; therefore, it could very well be one to three years. This is confirmation for when his career transition will take place.

Over the next few months, we continued to work together with Intuitive-Reiki sessions. Mandeep continued to lose weight, feel better, save money, and see some progress in his business financial situation. He kept on track with the tips and tools I had provided him and he was taking responsibility in his healing journey. His superpower icon is Iron Man. Mandeep loves this superhero and was able to visualize the Iron Man suit quickly.

What I have found from working with my male clients is that you love your superheroes, just as my sons do; therefore, it is easy for you to identify with one of them when flexing your intuitive muscle. The iconic superhero of another client of mine—whose favourite service is Reiki and who is journeying on the self-healing path—is Wolverine, who completely heals himself after getting injured.

Getting back to Mandeep, he was grateful for the Reiki he received. I told him rattlesnake animal spirit was with him, as he was going through a period of shedding old habits, old patterns, transforming, and becoming Iron Man. He laughed. Another happy client!

Journal Notes

_____
_____
_____
_____
_____
_____
_____
_____
_____
_____
_____
_____
_____
_____
_____
_____
_____
_____
_____
_____
_____
_____
_____
_____
_____
_____
_____
_____
_____
_____

Clairaudience—Can You Hear Me?

"All great men are gifted with intuition. They know without reasoning or analysis, what they need to know."
Alexis Carrel

Moving down the aisle in the tool department, we have "clairaudience," the sense that allows you to hear clearly with your supersonic ears. The online dictionary gives this definition for clairaudience, "The power to hear sounds said to exist beyond the reach of ordinary experience or capacity, as the voices of the dead."

I explain clairaudience as the voice that you hear within your head. As with clairvoyance, clairaudience is hearing interior and exterior voices, sounds and noises. Daily, we hear many voices and much mind chatter going through our heads. Most of the time, we are trying to quiet them; now, I am asking you to listen to them.

Many of my clients find this sense the most challenging due to the constantly cluttered state of their minds. A cluttered mind is a messy state of disorganized thoughts, feelings, and perceptions that waste time and take up too much space. A cluttered mind does not serve a useful purpose; it is an obstruction, a roadblock to your intuition, to your gut instincts. Mind chatter is when you go through your to-do list; wonder what you are going to eat for dinner; ask yourself questions such as "Did I forget to turn off the stove?"; think of calling your mother; wonder what your kids are doing in school; or—my personal favourite—beat yourself up for not listening to your gut instincts!

Why is the mind chatter from a cluttered mind detrimental

to flexing your intuitive muscle? The answer is simple. It will prevent you from focusing on your goals; you will have difficulty making key business decisions; you will forget important and pertinent details for closing the next deal; you will experience less joy and peace in your work and in your home life; you will lack creativity and productivity; you might get a splitting migraine; you could be angry; you might be unable to sleep. Mind chatter makes your intuitive muscle flabby!

The first thing on the agenda is to learn how to recognize the voices that reside in your head and to weed out the ones you do not need to listen to because they serve no purpose. With so many external sounds all about, how can you easily distinguish between your intuitive tool of clairaudience and all the other voices, one of them being yours? Just as you learned to ride a bicycle or to recognize the different tools in the garage, you'll learn to identify which voice is whose, which language is being spoken, and which noises and sounds need to be heard. Sound easy? (Pun intended.)

Numero uno important point to know is that the voice of intuition—your supersonic hearing—will never speak in anger or fear. It will present itself in a calm demeanour and possibly with firmness. I say firmness, because you might need to hear the message more than once or even all of a sudden in order to avoid an accident. The information that you hear will be useful.

Second in importance is how you hear it. If you hear an "I" such as "I must…," "I should…," "I am…," "I, I, I…," this is probably yourself talking to yourself. For example, you might say to yourself, "I am hungry…," "I am thirsty…," whereas your superpower clairaudient tool will use your name or "You" when this sense is active. In this case, it might sound a bit like the following, "You must turn right here." "You should check in on your dad." "Jack, did you hear that?" "Rob, pay attention!"

This means your spidey-hearing will give you an action that you must do and you will continue to hear it until you carry out those actions, or you may eventually stop hearing it, because you choose to ignore the messages. Albeit, beware of the consequences of your nonactions following from hearing clairaudience, or you will experience an "in hindsight" moment.

Lastly, pay attention to the outside world. A subtle whisper, a loud crash, a high-pitched noise, overhearing a conversation, and hearing your name being called out may all be signs to grab your attention. Too often, we discard what is repeating itself in our head, be it a musical lyric, the name of a friend we haven't connected with in a long time, or a new business idea percolating. Anything you hear that seems to have meaning probably does.

SITTING ON THE EDGE OF MY SEAT

I recall back to my childhood when I was about nine years old. My grandfather and I were rocking on chairs one warm summer evening. He sat with an apple in one hand and a paring knife in the other. He would ask me what I heard. I'd laugh and reply, "You are so silly, Grandpapa. I can hear you talking to me now."

Over his glasses, he'd respond with a very serious tone. "My little girl, I want you to listen deeply to the sounds around and tell me what you hear."

As he cut a piece of apple and ate it, I sat in silence and listened intently. He waited patiently eating his apple as I wondered if I would get a piece of his delicious fruit. Moments later, he'd look over and ask again, "What do you hear, Michèle?"

I wanted to make him proud and I hoped I heard what he wanted me to hear when I answered, "I can hear the wind blowing through the leaves on the trees."

"This is good, little girl; continue listening, Michèle," and he rewarded me with a piece of apple.

I moved to the edge of my seat and heard my grandfather tell me to relax and not try so hard to hear the noises. He persisted in telling me to just let the sounds naturally flow to my ears. Rocking in my chair, I allowed my awareness of the noises to heighten. I was amazed at what I could hear. I suddenly looked over to my grandfather knowing he would be satisfied with my answer. He sat in silence, smiled, holding another piece of apple; he was ready to hand it over to me.

I said, "I could hear the grass grow, Grandpapa."

He passed me the piece of apple and congratulated me with a job well done. We carried on this way until sunset and it was time for me to go home.

My grandfather and I had several occasions to spend afternoons such as this one together when he would teach me how to really listen and pay attention to the world around me. My grandfather was a pillar in educating me on how to flex my intuitive muscles. I say muscles, because you will learn that there are many different ways our intuition flexes. He taught me to spark each of my senses to their fullest degree and I am grateful for our lasting relationship as his spirit continues to guide me.

ॐ CLAIRAUDIENCE EXERCISE

Sit comfortably listening to classical music and try to identify the many instruments you hear. You don't need to know exactly what the name of each instrument is; rather, try to identify how many appear in the song.

You can also do the exercise my grandfather had me do on the porch. Sit and listen to all the sounds around you and identify them. The sound of traffic, a bird chirping, the kids playing in the street, the airplane flying by, the television in the next room, the wind blowing outside, and so on. Notice what you hear with each ear separately and where the noise is coming from, from the right, from behind, or from afar. This is a type of open-monitoring meditation as you sit and listen to each sound you hear without being attached to it. You simply hear it, acknowledge it, and move on to the next sound. Eventually, your clairaudient tool will be so sharp that you'll be surprised when you hear what you were meant to hear and you act upon it instantly.

Client Story #2—Don't Take Your Motorcycle Today!

Adam is an average guy with a regular job and a family. He has been working in the same industry for over twenty-four years and likes his work. He loves spending time with his children by volunteering in their various activities. Adam would tell you that he is not an intuitive man, as he has doubted and over-thought his superpower most of his life. Adam did nothing to flex his intuitive muscle other than occasionally listen to his wife's stories of intuition. He insisted that he believed her, since he could see how authentic she was when she shared her intuitive adventures. Yet, Adam's intuitive muscle was flabby and out of shape. Over the years of listening to his wife's experiences, his own spidey-senses became more apparent.

When Adam came to me, his intention was to stop the mind chatter. He confessed it was troublesome to stop the many thoughts flowing through his head—they stressed him out. It also caused him to be an impatient man and at times to feel angry. He would describe his feelings of anger as a pressure cooker, never really sure when it would explode.

I suggested he start with a short breathing meditation. He found the meditation very easy to follow, and was able to completely zone out and quiet his mind. I gave him a few more tips on how to use his clairaudient tool. Adam found that his intuition spoke to him more often and more frequently.

I questioned him whether—when he heard it—he did indeed follow through with his inner Voodoo voice. He revealed to me that he did not follow through every time and he regretted each instance. Yet, he stated that when he followed what his clairaudient tool told him, he never knew whether indeed it had been correct.

We chatted about this in greater detail. I asked him to think of the alternative of not following through with the intuitive voice he heard. What did he think would happen? He professed, "How can we be one-hundred percent sure?"

I responded, "I don't think you'll ever know; however, I suspect the alternative would not be for your greatest good."

At least, Adam agreed to this. His curiosity got the best of him one morning when he did not listen to the intuitive voice in his head giving him advice. This is what happened.

His early morning day started as most of them did. He woke up at 5:00 a.m. to get to work for a 6:00 a.m. shift. It was a warm July morning and the weather forecast was calling for temperatures over eighty degrees and sun all day. He thought to himself, "Why not take my motorcycle to work today?"

As he was gathering his motorcycle gear of gloves, boots, leather jacket, and helmet, he suddenly heard, "Do not take your bike today!" The voice stopped him in his tracks. "Why would I not take my bike to work today?" he reasoned with himself. Securing his lunch box on his motorcycle, he again heard more intently, "Do not take your bike today!"

"Why not?" he shouted back in his mind. "How often do I get to ride my motorcycle anymore? I am so busy with the kids." Continuing to reason with himself, he thought, "It'll be such a nice ride into work this morning: no traffic, the sun rising, the warm air. Screw it; I'm taking my motorcycle. What is the worst thing that could happen?"

As Adam pulled out of his garage, driving away to the stop sign, he heard for the last time, "Do not take your bike!" Rather than turning around, returning back home, and changing his mode of transportation, Adam carried on riding his motorcycle.

Once Adam was almost over the bridge, a passerby tried to grab his attention. The stranger finally succeeded, yelled something that Adam couldn't hear, and pointed to the back of his motorcycle. Shrugging his shoulders, Adam waved and rode on. Arriving at the next street light, he decided to check out what the man was trying to communicate to him. Placing his bike on its stand, he moved around to the back of his motorcycle only to notice his licence plate was gone along with the bracket that had been holding it in place.

He couldn't help but laugh at this bizarre situation. His intuition was trying to warn him prior to leaving the house to not take his motorcycle, yet Adam chose to ignore it and stated reasons why he should take his bike.

When he shared this story with me, he asked with sincerity, "How am I supposed to know the difference between my telling myself what I should do and my intuitive muscle flexing?"

I explained to Adam to pay attention to what the voice is saying and how it is speaking. Over time with practice, he would learn easily and quickly to differentiate the two—his own everyday thoughts and his very own bionic ear, his clairaudient tool.

In a recent conversation with Adam, he informed me that he can now easily recognize when it is his clairaudient tool working rather than his own thoughts. He said I'd be proud of him, because he listened to his intuition speaking to him just the other day. This is what happened.

Once again riding his motorcycle on a particularly warm, early spring day, Adam was coming home from work; he stopped at the streetlight enjoying the air on his face. All of a sudden, a man pulled up beside Adam, rolled down his window, and advised him not to go straight through on this road because there was a speed trap up ahead. Adam noticed that the man only spoke to him and no one else. He thought this bizarre at first. Why would a complete stranger only advise him? Rather than thinking this man and the situation at hand were peculiar,

Adam chose to listen to his intuitive tool that came through this total stranger. He was not worried about speeding as he didn't speed, although he had a feeling that it would be best to turn left at the lights and avoid the speed trap. Obviously, the rest of his ride home went smoothly.

Adam said to me, "I guess I'll never know if I would have gotten hassled on my bike that afternoon. What I can assure you is that it all turned out well in the end. So I never know how my clairaudient tool of intuition will speak to me. I now know to be ready to listen and pay attention."

Adam indicated recently he is so comfortable using this tool that he shared this story with one of his co-workers. At first, he said it felt strange to be talking about his intuition with another man, until he quickly realized his co-worker was more in line with his own intuitive muscle than Adam was. My client was amazed. So now alongside the "What about those Habs?" conversations, they can discuss (not all the time) their personal intuitive insights and learn from one another.

I applaud Adam for growing his tool of intuition; he is much more apt to pay attention, listen, and act on it. Good on you, Adam!

Journal Notes

Clairsentience—*Feel Me Up*, Please

"*Feel the force.*"
Yoda

Grab your next tool, "clairsentience," meaning to feel and sense emotions. Each man, woman, and child loves to feel and to be felt. We use touch frequently throughout our daily lives. I am touching each key as I type. I feel they are smooth and cool. When I am introduced to a new client, I shake their hand. I can feel his warm, strong hand. When my boys arrive home from school, I greet them with a tender embrace and a kiss on the cheek. I can feel the softness of their bodies as we hug, I can feel the coolness of the outdoors on their cheeks, and they can feel my arms wrapping around their waists.

My point is that we are constantly touching something or someone.

Clairsentience works much the same way as we physically touch our way through life. This tool will present itself in many different forms for each person. Some of you may feel pressure on various parts of your body, such as your head or your chest. You may feel cool or warm air around you. Other feelings may include external goose bumps that you can see on your arms or internal ones that you can only feel inside your arms. Clairsentience may feel like shivers down your spine or at the back of your neck. Some feelings involve sweating, brief aches, tightness, headaches, clenching of your fists or jaw, and even nausea if you might be making the wrong choice. Or you may feel lightness, you may begin to smile and laugh, or have an overall sense of goodness in your stomach, your gut, when the choice is clearly the right one to venture upon.

Often when an individual is sensitive or empathic toward others around him, he may get a sense of their projected emotions and interpret them as belonging to himself when in fact they don't. It is critical for you to identify when this happens.

For instance, you may be in a cheery mood until you arrive home from work. Your wife has been home all day with no one to talk to and is in a foul mood. As you walk through the door, she immediately charges at you, and starts to blurt out what has made her mood shift. All of a sudden, your happy frame of mind becomes foul. You have taken on too many of her emotions as your own, rather than safeguarding yourself.

At times, it is fine to feel a bit of what anyone is projecting, as it can be beneficial for you too. Just as laughter is contagious, so is every other emotion. Some dispositions are good to catch, such as happiness, joy, peace, excitement, and calm. Yet most of us don't want to feel another's fear, anger, depression, or other low emotions.

This would be similar to in the movie *Hancock*, in which the main character, who is immortal, and the female immortal were drawn to each other over many lifetimes, despite centuries and distance keeping them apart. Incidentally, they also drained each other's powers when in the presence of one another; therefore, we can say they are clairsentient or empathetic.

Getting back to the situation about the modern-day wife, you may want to step back a little, breathe deeply, and project your cheery mood back to her. This will act as a barrier so you can remain clear-headed when you are listening to her problem. Try not to fix her problem; do not offer solutions or your opinion, as she probably wants you only to listen. Besides, if you offer solutions you may very well be ignoring your happy emotional state. Now, try *feeling up* your clairsentience. How does it feel when you remain in your happy place and send that energy out to your wife? You may sense a bit of her emotions without taking too much of them on and she will become much happier because you have listened to her.

You can try to experiment with different scenarios involving sensations from other people's moods. A word of caution: if you are getting too emotionally charged or experience mood swings, stop until you have sought out the assistance of someone like me who can properly support you and teach you the necessary techniques to keep yourself safe.

But let's keep it really simple. Try the next exercise in discovering your clairsentient strength.

ॐ CLAIRSENTIENCE EXERCISE

Walk barefoot in the grass, in the sand, or in a body of water and feel every blade, every grain, or every drop of the water flowing around your feet, below them, and in between your toes. Get a sense of the temperature, the texture, and if there are any obstacles or other objects within the medium you are feeling. Try the same exercise with your hands. Touch different materials from rough sandpaper to smooth glass. This simple and easy exercise will bring more awareness to what you can feel and sense around you.

Why would this tool of clairsentience be useful? Think of when you are in the market to buy a house. How does it feel to walk over the threshold of the house? Do you get a sense and a feeling that the house is a happy place or not? When you are looking for collaborative partnerships in business, what emotions do you feel emanating from your potential partner? Do you feel as though you can trust him or her? What are the natural signs your body is providing in this moment that give you acumen and wisdom in order to trust or not trust the situation at hand?

CLIENT STORY #3—"DO YOU FEEL ME?"

John came to me at a crossroads in his life. His marriage had just fallen apart for no real reason, he thought, and his work environment was a hostile one-way street. He told me that he felt drained at the end of his workday, even when he sleeps a full eight hours the night before. John explained he does not feel the same on his days off or when he needs to be off-site for work. He enjoys walking the beach with his dogs to relax, loves to play sports with his best buddy, and travels every chance he gets.

John originally came to see me for a Reiki treatment, as per the suggestion of another client of mine, who is in the business of assisting individuals as a spiritual counsellor. She had recommended my exceptional ability to guide people through personal transformation. John was curious about Reiki, what it was, what it did, and he knew little about it. He loved his first session so much that he quickly booked three more within the month.

What John enjoyed the most about the Reiki treatments was how he felt afterwards. He stated he could feel heat radiating from my hands during the session. What fascinated John over the course of his sessions with me was how I could pick up on his energy when he just lay on his back with his eyes closed, without saying a word.

He always wondered how I was able to read him so easily. I explained to him that I simply picked up on the thoughts and feelings he was projecting and undergoing. John expressed great satisfaction in my guiding him to lead a more inspired life by taking the right measures in clearing his blocked energy.

Furthermore, John said he felt like a child again; he wanted to go out and have fun! I inquired as to what "fun" would look like for him, because I could tell he had been neglecting the child within. He wasn't sure yet. That evening, John went shopping and bought himself a longboard, which is similar to a skateboard, just longer in length, allowing the rider more precision to slide and skid down a paved road. He hadn't ridden one before and was feeling quite exhilarated with his purchase. Arriving home, he put on his protective gear and took his new longboard out for a ride on a neighbourhood street with a great incline. John felt free, at ease, and had so much fun, just like he had as a child.

During his next treatment, he spoke of his purchase and how the Reiki session ignited his inner child and he remembered to take time to amuse himself. John expressed gratitude for the Reiki treatments and their magical power of helping him flex, trust, and follow his intuitive muscle by engaging in the joys of life more frequently.

At one Reiki treatment, John felt a strong electrifying pulse emanating from my hands while I was working on an ache he had in his neck and shoulders. John had been experiencing severe headaches and tension in his shoulders due to a buildup of stress from his work environment. After his Reiki session, we chatted as to why he thought his work situation caused these adverse effects that manifested as headaches and shoulder pain. He felt as though he was working in an unappreciative and fear-based environment where employees were constantly threatened about their jobs and given only the slightest positive feedback. In the long run, John physically felt sick to his stomach each day at work. Shortly after his workday had finished and he sat comfortably at the beach with his dogs, his feelings of stress and nausea would subside.

I asked John a poignant question to which the answer seemed obvious to me. "Why do you continue to work in a place that causes you great discomfort and leaves you feeling ill at the end of the day?" He confessed that he could not trust his feelings anymore to recognize a better workplace; when he went for job interviews, his body would tighten and he would feel a sensation of the room closing in on him. John knew that his clairsentient tool was rusty.

Over the course of a few months, John continued his Reiki treatments with me, alongside guidance I provided for him to flex his intuitive muscle. He was dedicated to finding a new work avenue and a relationship with a partner within the year. Through our sessions together, John was able to reignite his clairsentient tool, his feelings. He was able to sense what it would feel like to work somewhere different with a new outlook on his professional career. John learned to trust and recognize his intuitive feelings during interviews. He knew that when he felt a stomach ache (not a nervous feeling or butterflies in his stomach)—a true ache he could easily identify as a pain projecting in his lower abdomen—this meant it would not be a good fit for employment for him. John was able to notice a numb-like feeling in his arms—they felt so heavy that he could barely move them. This indicated a neutral feeling toward the workplace. He knew this place of employment would not be stressful; yet it would not bring him a sense of great joy either.

Continuing the interview process, he finally felt something he hadn't felt in a long time. He explained to me that he could only describe it as something he feels when he travels. John loves to travel. Travelling brings him a great deal of joy, comfort, and happiness. When he thinks of travelling, John always smiles as he did throughout this particular interview.

I looked him straight in the eye and asked the ever-burning question, "What was the outcome of this interview?"

He sat smiling and nodding his head; he had been offered the position and he had accepted. We both contemplated he had travelled toward an inward journey that led to positive results in his career.

I saw John and his dogs a few months later, as my husband and I walked the beach. John expressed how happy he was in his new position. He was grateful for the opportunity to have taken time to travel prior to beginning his employment with them, to rest, recharge, and relax. His new employment soon brought him the opportunity to travel overseas. John was thrilled and he was beaming as he shared this information with me and my husband. After our walk on the beach, watching the dogs playfully run about as the sun was setting, we three wished each other a fabulous weekend and waved, "Bye for now."

Journal Notes

_____
_____
_____
_____
_____
_____
_____
_____
_____
_____
_____
_____
_____
_____
_____
_____
_____
_____
_____
_____
_____
_____
_____
_____
_____
_____
_____
_____
_____
_____

Claircognizance—You Know It, Baby!

"Trust instinct to the end, even though you can give no reason."
Ralph Waldo Emerson

Another important tool to have on your belt is "claircognizance," which is defined as clear knowing of what is about to occur in the future or may have occurred in the past. This tool can assist you when making critical and everyday decisions regarding situations or people in your life. It is typically what you men use most often, yet you don't even realize or associate it with your intuition. This is your true gut instinct flexing at its best. You just know it and you just do it! There is no scientific proof, no evidence to back it up. You don't see it, you don't hear it, and you don't feel it. You simply know it! Like magic, poof, it just appears in your mind, in your thoughts, and you know it to be true without a doubt.

Do you recognize the following sentence when this tool is at work for you? "Don't ask me how I know; I just do." This tool is also, by far, the one most of my clients have a challenge gaining confidence with. Watch out when the confidence builds, because it is super powerful and accurate. Your gut instinct, your claircognizant tool can be easily recognized.

How do you know what you know? Let me show you how simple it is to interpret this sense in your daily life. You are busy doing your work, whatever it is you do best. You are thinking critically, you are focused, you are analytical, and you are in control. All of a sudden, out of the blue, appears a thought—the greatest idea that is absolutely unrelated to what you are doing in this very moment. This thought potentially has considerable relevance and insight to a burning question you might have been pondering days before regarding an upcoming business transaction. Do not let that thought go! Hang on to it, write it down, memo it to yourself on your iPhone, or send yourself a voicemail. If you do not follow through and use the claircognizant promptings properly and immediately, you'll suffer from the "In hindsight, I should have..." syndrome.

I will venture to say, it'll be even stronger from now on, because you are better equipped than you were when you began reading this book. It'll be as though you got kicked in the groin, because it'll hurt so intensely and the regret will be grave.

What is the "In hindsight, I should have, I could have..." syndrome? This is my definition for this pain-in-the-arse syndrome: it is when you ask, think, ponder for guidance and clarity on a particular topic/issue/situation in your life (whether for personal or business use), and you actually receive an answer; yet, you choose to ignore it, not trust it, doubt it, wait too long to act upon it, and so forth. In that instant, you'll slap yourself on the forehead and shout out a big fat, "Shit! I knew it! I should have...!"

Or perhaps, you knew not to do business with a particular company and you chose to anyway, and now you regret it. Furthermore, hindsight is when you reconsider your present actions based on past knowledge, but it is too late to change or course-correct, since the moment has already escaped. Now that the situation is past, you have the information you needed to make a different decision. You may have had claircognizance of what to do, yet chose to ignore or not give it the attention it deserved; in this moment, it no longer serves you. You will regret your present actions, because you had the foresight beforehand to make the correct choice. Remember to trust the powerful and empowering information your gut gives you throughout the day. Do not let your intuitive judgment be clouded by your mind and overthink what you know.

The very popular sentence—"In hindsight, I should have…"—can unequivocally be avoided if you follow your gut instincts! Don't let this happen to you again. Follow your gut, your superpower tool, your claircognizance! You will most likely not experience an "in hindsight" moment again.

ॐ Claircognizance Exercise

If you know you've had a claircognizant thought or idea, re-member when it came to you in the first place, try to think back to what occurred right before, during, and immediately afterwards. Pinpoint every detail of how you felt, what you noticed, and what was happening around you. Become more aware; engage your powers of observation. This will make it easier to establish when this tool is working at its best for you. Write down everything you can recall and keep it in a safe place to refer to later.

This is not necessarily the easiest thing to do at first, because you'll probably be thinking too much with your mind. Beyond a shadow of a doubt, I do not doubt that you will think to yourself, "Is that what was happening when this thought came to the forefront or was it…?" Try, try to not think this way. You will not be successful with this exercise if you doubt.

Simply grab your pen and allow the words to flow automatically. It might be easier to start with a sentence such as, "This is silly …" or "I will remember what I need to remember…" or "I don't know what I know, I just know…" Starting in this fashion will prevent you from overthinking and will organically begin the process of mechanical and robotic writing. Before you know it, you will have written a few paragraphs, a page, or more. Then, go ahead and read what you've written. I must stress to keep this exercise simple and fun. Do not concern yourself with grammar, punctuation, and spelling. This will allow the words to flow naturally and to roll off your pen. Afterwards, you will be more in tune with when your claircognizant thought occurs. You'll be better equipped to just know what you know. You may actually surprise yourself and instead of saying, "Oh, shit, I should have ...," you'll be proudly proclaiming with a high five, "I just knew it, man, and I did it!"

Client Story # 4—My Gut Is My Gauge for What's Right and Wrong

Lance and I have known each other for a few years. He is my neighbour. As we were getting to know one another during one fine summer's day, Lance realized that I was the woman he had questioned about the neighbourhood months before when he was house hunting. We became friendly neighbours immediately as both our families love spending time outdoors and our kids play together on the block. We would talk for hours on end about the kids, our days at work, our plans for the summer, our families, and life in general.

Lance is a fairly active guy who enjoys playing racquetball at least three times a week and painting nature scenes. He is a divorced dad who savours every moment during the day interacting with his children, as they live with him on a full-time basis. He has not found it easy to adjust to the divorce and he continues to be involved in the day-to-day activities of his children. He is a dedicated father who travels monthly for his work. When he is away from home, he calls his children every night to check in, get the "Coles Notes" of their day, and wish them a good night.

I noticed in our conversations that Lance appeared to be relatively in tune with his intuition, in particular his claircognizant tool, despite his analytical, business, pragmatic mind. This is why we have so much in common, as my mind works the same way. We can both easily be in the creative sides of our minds when we are in an artistic mood. As I mentioned, Lance paints amazingly beautiful nature scenes. He needed to give himself more credit, I noticed. I made sure that when each piece was either in progress or finished, I commented on how serene and realistic his art is. I think he still owes me a piece for my living room wall, since I absolutely adore his work!

Getting back to his instincts, he'd often say, "My gut led me to …," "I just it knew it was the right time to do…" One day, I decided to invite Lance to try out one of my services, as he found them curious and fascinating. He did confess he had a few highly intuitive friends himself, although he didn't think he was intuitive at all. I begged to differ. Sitting over tea and coffee on Lance's back porch, I gave him the lowdown on what a typical session of mine looks like. Lance was inquisitive and responded positively to working together. We arranged our first session for the next day.

Lance holds a management position in a very busy firm in the building industry. He is quite content with his profession, his employer, and his team. His work is fast-paced, requires much clarity, keen productivity, and excellent people skills, all of which Lance possesses and then some.

One evening while we walked our dogs and watched our respective children riding their bikes ahead of us, Lance stated that lately he had been feeling as though a change would occur in his work environment. I confirmed his thought. He inquired, "How do you do that? How can you just know?"

I briefly explained to him how my intuitive information flows easily through words I hear, through images and symbols I see, or, in this case, I just know something to be true. Lance was impressed and was enthusiastic for his one-on-one session.

He announced to me during our first session that he had just been offered a new position with a different firm, which would entail much more travel as part of his responsibilities. Lance laughed a little while stating, "You already knew that, didn't you?"

I smiled and continued to listen attentively. Most of the

travel would be throughout British Columbia plus many nights in Ontario. He seemed excited with the new change, yet apprehensive, as this would mean less time with his children. We discussed the pros and cons of some of the new responsibilities: taking on an additional team and overlooking the new office. Lance seemed quite level-minded as he pondered his choice and acknowledged he is too much in his head at the moment to make a clear, well-balanced decision. Lance sought guidance in other domains of his life as we moved along with the session.

Another pressing issue was his love life. It has been a few years since his divorce finalized. He had been dating a few women, nothing serious. He felt as though it was time to move on. Lance was finding this to be quite challenging, particularly with his youngest son. Despite the fact that his ex-wife was not too involved in their lives, Lance still felt a sense of loyalty to the mother-child bond. He realized that it would seem odd to his children to have their dad date another woman.

Overall, I felt Lance had been very protective of his children and had most certainly been an *utmost gentleman* during the courting period. He was selective and had only been on a handful of dates. I urged Lance to get out there. Eventually, Lance did meet a kind-hearted, responsible, like-minded woman. They decided to date and by the third date, they realized this could become a serious relationship.

Throughout this period, Lance wanted to know what I thought, intuitively, of his new girlfriend. I had not met her. I asked Lance for her name. I closed my eyes and saw a woman who was gentle, loving, caring, and had the potential to be his equal partner in their relationship. I advised Lance to just go with his gut as he had done in the past. I asked him to notice what his gut was communicating to him.

"What does your claircognizant tool know for sure about this woman?" Lance pondered this and was pleased with the intuitive answers, tips, tools, and exercises that I gave him to work on until our next meeting.

During our next appointment, Lance requested Reiki. He had never heard of Reiki before meeting me and wanted the "scoop" on how it worked. I gave him some background as to how Reiki had been discovered, how it came to be present in the Eastern World, its benefits, and my explanation of how it works. Lance was interested to know how Reiki would feel and if he might gain further insight on his decision to move ahead with the job offer, plus gain more clarity with his budding relationship.

After his Reiki treatment, Lance was thrilled to say he felt a new sense of aliveness, a feeling of being refreshed, and a newfound energy level that had been missing before. He had been so preoccupied with the finite details of the new offer that he felt depleted, uncreative, sluggish, and tired. Although he had been practising his sport, it felt like a chore to go out three times a week during his career transition. I strongly advised Lance to let go of the decision-making process and stop thinking about it for a few days. He had been overthinking and I asked him to take a break. With a perplexed look, he questioned how he was to do this. I told him to concentrate simply on what he was doing at the moment and to be fully engaged in that activity, whether it was painting, playing racquetball, playing with the kids, or cooking dinner. I advised him to trust me and I comically added, "Haven't I always been correct and accurate with the information I have given you in the past?" I proceeded to advise him that his answers would come through so crystal clearly that they would throw him off his game, literally speaking!

I am pleased to report that the answer came to Lance as clear as day while he was intently playing racquetball. He declared, "I just knew I had to take the new job!" He did indeed accept the new management position.

On the love front, Lance is still dating the woman of his dreams. They are madly in love, just as he "knew" he would be by the third date. His gut had told him so. Their children have met one another and Lance's youngest son is coming around. He is realizing that this new woman has her own children and is not there to replace his mom. Simply put, Lance is another happy client!

Journal Notes

Part Two
I Know Tim Will Die; Where's My Inner Voodoo Shit?

Tim's Journey

"Whatever life holds in store for me, I will never forget these words: 'With great power comes great responsibility.' This is my gift, my curse. Who am I? I'm Spider-man."
Peter Parker

Eventually, my husband was repeating what I sensed and predicted to myself about his death, though not in so many words. He would often tell the boys that if they stressed him out too much, he'd die of a heart attack before the age of forty-five. His gut was preparing him for his death. I'd get so annoyed with these statements and suggest he not place such guilt on our children. Such comments as this and others would send me to a reflective state where I questioned whether or not I wanted to continue my relationship with my husband. I was feeling rather unhappy and I could see that Tim was no happier. When I would think of remaining married to my husband, my body felt tight. I would switch my thinking to being separated, and my body immediately felt light—the tension in my shoulders eased. I knew it was time to speak my truth and have a conversation with Tim, which I knew was not going to be easy.

One sunny afternoon, I confessed that we had been distant and disconnected, and I hadn't felt the love or the spark we once had. I was tired of trying to save him. Ouch! That hurt! Tim was not thrilled. There were of course other factors in our relationship we discussed that ultimately led to our separation.

In the end, we separated for a few months. I finally felt a huge *weight lift off my chest*. During the last few months preceding our separation, I felt as though an elephant was sitting on my chest making it onerous to breathe. I felt as though I could never fill my lungs to capacity. I questioned why, as I meditate regularly and practise yoga daily. I am very cognizant of what the breath does to our physical, emotional, and energetic bodies. It is an essential part of our being. To breathe is to live. To breathe is to allow the energy to pulse within us. Our breath provides vitality, oxygen, and blood flow to our organs, including our lungs, and mine seemed to be depriving themselves of oxygen lately. What I know to be the absolute truth today is my gut instincts were giving me a small sign of what was to come.

We physically separated in the fall and somewhat reconciled in the New Year.

During a meditation in January 2013, I again heard, "Tim will die now, even though he is happy."

Hearing this, I got upset with my intuition, my superpower, my gift, my curse, my guidance, Angels, spirits, God, the Universe, Supreme Power, whatever the hell was out there, greater than us. I cursed them all! I thought what an effing cruel joke! This is how this gift can be a curse at least for me: the foreknowledge of a death.

Not entirely doubting my gut, I sat and waited (once again). I did negotiate with myself that I would no longer fear this vision. I surrendered; I let the thought go; I gave up. I was determined to live whatever time Tim and I had left together, being happier and not thinking about his death. "God," if you will, was in charge. While rebuilding our marriage, I went about my everyday routines with my business and my family, until…

THE DREADED DAY IS UPON US

It was Sunday, February 3, 2013 when Tim arrived home from work and stated he felt a cold coming on. He decided to stay home from work the following day to rest and fight the cold. In the days that followed, Tim stayed home while the boys went to school and I went to work. No need to worry, I told myself as my husband demonstrated regular flu-like symptoms. In this moment of living life with the hustle and bustle, the thought never occurred to me that this was "his" time. Or, was I in denial of my vision of his death that was creeping up fast?

By the third day of Tim's "cold," I asked him if he felt weird and strange as he was displaying odd behaviour. He replied that he did indeed feel bizarre and this cold or flu felt abnormally different from others in the past. Specifically, he had trouble sleeping (which does not typically happen during the flu), as he kept hearing buzzing, drumming, ringing-types of noises in his ears. I inquired if he had heard them before; he answered no. He explained that his dreams were equally peculiar with lines and numbers that he could not understand flowing by. He informed me that the noises, lines, and numbers kept recurring throughout the day, and he struggled with his thoughts.

In a lucid moment, Tim drove himself to a doctor's appointment and was diagnosed with Influenza A. The signs pointed in that direction and he was told to take some time off from work to recuperate. The doctor indicated that he'd feel like crap for at least two to six weeks, suffering from fever, chills, sweats, coughing, and headaches.

When I arrived home from work on the fifth day of Tim's illness, there was a smell in the house that I could not describe. I had never smelled such an odour before. If I were to name it, I'd say that it smelled of death. You'd think I would recognize that this was a sign! A particular "clair," which I did not mention earlier in the book, is clairscence, which is clear smelling of either a spirit or of another person's energy or an illness. Because I was pissed at my intuition, God, or whatever, or whoever was in control of our destiny, I didn't think twice about this smell. Yet I did feel a slight nudge in my gut to reconsider and be more attentive. I had completely and fully surrendered, and temporarily forgotten about my vision of Tim's death.

So he could rest, I bought Tim some sleeping pills as per his request because his sleep pattern was off. Finally, for the first time in five days he slept a bit. I woke up with a start in the wee hours of the morning to hear Tim talking to me. I glanced at the clock and it read 4:00 a.m. Tim said he was going to work to drop off his sick notice to his boss. Feeling drowsy and confused from sleep, I asked him if he was fine to drive. He replied that he was and left.

Thirty minutes later, tossing and turning, I realized what had materialized. Now my intuition was screaming at me! He could get in a car accident driving in his sickly state. My goodness, what was I thinking, letting him go off in the middle of the night? Obviously, due to my sleep state, I hadn't fully realized what Tim was doing. I thought it was a dream. I forced myself to wake up as I started pacing the living-room floor. Minutes later, I was ready to dial his cell phone when the front door opened and Tim walked in. I questioned where he'd been. He said he had tried to drive to work to give his supervisor his sick note. It wasn't a dream! We both looked at each other stunned that he would attempt such a drive in his sick state, especially considering that his mental condition was off, to say the least. Before reaching the highway, Tim had speculated that driving in his condition was neither safe nor smart. We were both relieved and went back to bed.

The next day was Saturday, February 9. I was scheduled to meet with a potential client. I told my semi-awake husband that I would be gone for no more than two hours. He could call upon the boys if he needed anything, to stay in bed, and to continue to rest up. Kissing him on the cheek, I saw him opening his glazed eyes and saying, "I love you."

That turned out to be the last time he would say that for a long while.

Our youngest son woke his dad up a couple of hours later and that is when all hell broke loose.

When I arrived home, I found my husband sitting on the front steps. He was barely coherent, extremely weak, suffering from constant chills, having difficulty breathing, and his skin was grey and discoloured. He also could not keep any liquids in his stomach. My son mentioned that, upon waking his dad, Tim had fallen out of bed and could hardly walk on his own. A family friend, Jeff, suggested that I take my husband to the hospital immediately, as he was not making sense when he spoke and his speech was slurred. I decided to call a medical clinic and inquire if my husband was displaying "regular" flu-like symptoms. The nurse was definite in indicating to bring him to the hospital as soon as possible due to his age—forty-four years old—and the fact that he was incoherent.

I went onto autopilot. I had no clue what the hell was going on. I questioned what type of flu this could be that had my husband in such a plight. The thought never crossed my mind that this could be the day of his death. Or was it that I did not want to acknowledge it? I was definitely in denial. I had heard of other people getting very sick from the flu and I simply chalked it up to a strain that he hadn't encountered before.

Tests in Emergency

"It turns out that our intuition is a greater genius than we are."
Jim Shepard

We arrive at Peace Arch Hospital in our hometown at 4:43 p.m. Within moments of entering the waiting room, my husband is seen by a triage nurse, assessed, and wheeled into the emergency room. He is in critical condition; they pronounce him to be an ICU (Intensive Care Unit) patient; another doctor is called in to tend to him. Tim is subjected to a battery of tests, which include (but is not limited to) blood tests, swabs, an X-ray, a CT scan, and a spinal tap. The doctor is trying to rule out any type of virus and infection, both common and uncommon. He asks me several times if we have travelled offshore or to any tropical island within the last six months. I reply no to all his questions about travel abroad.

During this time, Tim is placed on an intravenous drip (an IV) that is filled with various antibiotics, multivitamins, and liquids. Now, I am getting worried. I need to remain calm as I can sense my husband's fear and distress. I need to safeguard myself from his emotions so I can remain levelheaded. I need my logical mind right now. I throw my intuition at the curb, thinking I do not need it at this moment. I need to focus and make rational decisions in order to save my husband's life.

Imagine, just months ago, I said to Tim I was done with saving him.

Yet, as I sit watching my husband struggle to breathe, my intuition kicks in, despite my trying to shut it down or at least tone it down a few notches. It reminds me to be attentive to the signs, to continue to use my powers of observation, to look for synchronicities, and to trust what is to come. With this newfound hope, I try to foresee the future of my husband's life. Nothing comes, no visions, no thoughts, no words, and no images. Darkness and cold are what I feel. No visions of rainbow colours. I feel utter nothingness and blackness.

"Is my intuition blocked?" I ask.

I hear a resounding, "No."

How can I decipher what I am feeling? What does the blackness mean?

Observing my husband as he falls in and out of consciousness, I affirm his spirit, his essence, his soul is leaving his body; therefore, what I am feeling is his empty shell, his physical almost lifeless body.

I determine it is best to connect with his parents; they live approximately four hours away by ferry; his father replies, "I will be there tomorrow."

I remain calm for my husband's sake, since I can see the uneasiness in his eyes when they are open. The doctor hasn't given me much information yet as he is still waiting for the multitude of test results to return. By 11:00 p.m., my husband's breathing is laboured and very deep. Fatigue is setting in for Tim; I suggest he try to rest, saying I will drive home quickly to check in with our three sons. It is quite perilous for me to leave my husband sleeping as I race home. I check for clarification with my intuition and the doctor to ensure this will not be the last time I see my husband alive. The doctor assures me Tim will be fine for a while and seems to be sleeping for now. My gut gives me the okay as well.

Once I arrive home, I tell our boys that their father and I will be in the hospital at least overnight. I kiss them each goodnight and direct our friend Jeff to come by the next morning. I see worry and anxiety in the children's eyes, as they do not understand what is happening to their dad. Then again, neither do I. I am shutting out the notion of my past vision of Tim's death. None of them ask if their dad is going to die and for that I am extremely grateful.

Upon returning to the hospital, one hour later, I see that my husband has an oxygen tube in his nose and the doctor briefs me on his pending decision to place my husband on life support. He explains that, with my husband's strained breathing, it would be best to intubate him to preserve his strength and allow healing to occur. Otherwise, we might be faced with a worsened state of health.

What are we healing? I wonder. We do not even know what we are dealing with. How do I explain to our children that their dad is on life support? I do not want to think of that now. Finally at 3:00 a.m., I fall asleep as Tim lingers on, slipping in and out of consciousness. Two hours later, I am awoken and we are moved to the ICU floor.

Now, my mind is racing and I no longer know what to think or feel. I am exhausted from the lack of sleep and I have a splitting migraine. (In retrospect, what was a migraine compared to Tim's suffering?) I still have no answers as to what has inflicted itself on my husband's health and the blackness carries on as I try to connect to my intuition. There are too many emotions flying around in a hospital to pinpoint exactly which ones are mine; also my skills are challenged by my tiredness and exhaustion. I remind myself of the tips and tools I repeatedly advise my clients to use in highly charged situations. I breathe in deeply through my nose and exhale with a sigh from my mouth. I am mindful of not breathing in this fashion in plain sight of my husband who is clearly still struggling to take a breath. I imagine his lungs filling readily with air as I pace, waiting for more news from the doctor.

Sunday, February 10, 2013—The Irony of the Breath

"My words, thoughts and deeds have a boomerang effect. So be careful what you send out!"
Allan Rufus

By the time we have transferred to the ICU ward, Tim's condition has drastically worsened. It is very early on Sunday, February 10, and I am running on fumes and adrenaline. I haven't had anything to eat or drink since breakfast on Saturday. We are both beyond fatigue and I suggest Tim try to sleep some more, despite the state of consciousness and unconsciousness he is enduring. He refuses. His eyes scream panic and horror as he is beginning to come to the reality of the seriousness of his condition. When I question him, he musters weakly that he is afraid of falling asleep.

I realize that his spidey-senses are in high gear, as are mine, despite the boxing match I am having with my intuition! I need it more than ever, yet I am too preoccupied with my rational mind to allow my intuition to take the lead. We both know that something is terribly wrong, and we have no definite answers.

He is even more incoherent; his breathing is deteriorating despite the oxygen, and he can barely stay awake. Tim fights to remain conscious and I try to reassure him that "everything is fine," despite not knowing a single damn thing. The doctor is becoming more and more concerned, and strongly recommends that I consider consenting to having Tim placed in a medically induced coma—basically, he would be put on life support. My gut tells me that this is indeed the best form of remedy for his survival.

It is important to have Tim understand—as best he can, considering his deteriorating condition—what would happen next. He seems to grasp the fact his life is at stake and his ailment is far worse than influenza. The doctor speaks directly to my husband and informs him that within thirty minutes, he will be placing him on life support in order to assist his breathing and the healing process. With all of his might, Tim whispers, "How long will I be sleeping?"

The doctor replies, "Our hope is three to four days."

He then proceeds to explain to me that it could be longer and he has a goal of taking my husband off life support within six or seven days, maximum. He alludes that when a patient is intubated for more than one week, the chances of survival are dramatically reduced as more infections can occur.

Now, I need to go home and explain to our children that indeed their dad will be on life support. I speak to the doctor and voice my concern that the boys would not be prepared for this; I ask if they could come by to visit their dad prior to his being placed in a medically induced coma. He answers that I need to hurry.

How do I prepare myself for this conversation? At least, when we announced our separation to the boys, we did it together and felt somewhat supported. This time is far different. The acknowledgement of doing this on my own is quickly sinking in. I vow to remain as calm and strong as possible for the sake of not alarming our boys.

I arrive home, sit the boys down, explain as best a mother can that their dad is extremely sick and we have no clue why, what has caused the illness, or even what the illness is.

Our youngest son, T.J., is devastated and begins to cry immediately. He shouts, "This is not fair, I don't like this, and I am going to be sad, forever!"

Memories of our separation come flooding back as T.J. meticulously echoes his thoughts and feelings.

Our other two boys Ross and Max sit in silence, stunned by the news and ask if they can visit their dad. I reply holding back tears, "Of course."

Ross speaks in a very mature tone, reassuring us that their dad will be fine. Max reiterates his older brother's sentiments by stating that with today's technology their dad will pull through. They say they feel this in their guts. "It will all be just fine, Maman," they whisper as they hug me, softly sobbing.

Fearing the worst and knowing that I need help, I immediately contact my mother in Ontario and bring her up to speed on the situation. She says that she will be on a plane tomorrow to stay and help take care of the boys.

Back at the hospital, my father-in-law has arrived while I have been to get the children. I fill him in with what little I know and the boys sit by their dad in a state of fear, uncertainty, and despair. They are very scared and worried now, seeing their dad so helpless and so uncomprehending, struggling with his breath, despite the oxygen mask he has been given.

Our older two boys who displayed such strength earlier at home begin to cry and fall apart. T.J. repeats how unfair this is, saying that besides, Family Day is coming up and this is not how we planned on spending the day! This man lying in the hospital bed does not resemble the man they know and love so dearly. The children say goodbye to their dad for now and promise to came back to visit tomorrow. My feeble and powerless husband musters the tenacity to reply softly, "I will see you boys when I wake up."

Standing as the pillar of strength for my family, I watch in silence as our children observe, give reassurance, and remain as composed as possible while encouraging their dad to get better soon. I feel proud of my young men as they display a spectrum of raw emotions from sadness and worry to certitude. It is ambiguous to not let your true emotions rise to the surface when you are faced with the potential death of a loved one, especially for young children. Regardless of Tim's weakness, he displays positivity in the health care system, faith and trust in the Universe, and delight in his children for taking care of their mom.

The boys return home with Jeff, who makes sure they are fed and kept busy. They have not seen their dad intubated yet and I dread the moment they will.

One hour prior to intubating Tim, a nurse places a central IV line in my husband. Moments before being intubated, fear fills Tim's eyes; he speaks faintly in a scared, yet inquisitive voice, "Will I dream?"

I answer, "Yes, you will. I love you. See you in a few days."

The doctor and the nurses ask me to leave the small space that comprises my husband's room in the ICU ward. Peace Arch Hospital is small and old; the ICU ward does not have traditional rooms with doors. The rooms have one small window, a tiny sink, two walls on either side, one facing the back, a bed in the centre, space for one visitor's chair, and, where the front wall should be, is an open space looking right at the nurses' station. There hangs a curtain if you want privacy, yet I am encouraged to leave it open at all times due to the critical nature of Tim's health. A monitor hanging in the back left corner tracks heartbeat and oxygen levels. I don't want to leave the ward although I know the doctor does not want me to observe the procedure of inserting a tube down my husband's throat.

I step off to the side, and sit in a chair by the nurses' station, peering what the doctor and the nurses are doing to my husband. Once the doctor detects I am there, he firmly insists that I leave the ward. I plead with the nurse sent to remove me by stating that I need to stay and that I am fine observing from a distance. It is difficult and surreal to watch my husband's lifeless body get intubated. I have a feeling of massive numbness come over me as I sit quietly, tears flowing from my eyes, with no thoughts of hope or fear. I am mirroring my husband's comatose state. My intuition seems to have shut down on purpose, perhaps for my sanity and protection.

In less than twenty-four hours of walking into the emergency room, my husband has been placed on life support.

We finally know he was in septic shock as a result of an acute infection. Septic shock occurs when your body is severely infected in one area and it begins to fail, one organ at a time. Sepsis is caused by a bacterial, fungal, or viral infection. Such infections can occur in the digestive system, urinary tract, or lungs, as in pneumonia. The mortality rate in patients with septic shock is over 50 percent. A patient will have a greater chance of survival depending on early detection of the infection, the fewer organs that have failed, and how quickly they receive treatment. One thing I inherently know is that if my husband were admitted to the hospital a day later, the outcome would have changed drastically.

Ladybugs are everywhere on the inside of the tiny window in my husband's so-called "room" of the ICU ward. I find nature speaks to us in mysterious ways, thus I make a note to find out the significance of "ladybug." They will have a message that fits this situation. Ladybug's spirit tells me to take time and meditate or to pray alone in quiet. I am doing that each day as I sit, watch my husband lie in the bed, and I write in a meditative state to release my stress and gain insight. Ladybug spirit also tells me that something I think I have lost will come back to me.

I ponder, what have I lost?

I have lost some of my loving and compassionate feelings toward my husband over the past year and most recently when we separated. I have currently lost my husband, as this body lying here is not completely and fully him. His physical body is lying on the bed; however, his spirit has departed for now. The message from "ladybug" is resonating true for this time of uncertainty. Tim is on his own journey and I hope it will be an enlightened adventure. My gut instincts are feeling quite the contrary. For Tim's sake, I wish him safe travel to wherever he needs to venture. I send him loving, light feelings of happiness and protection through my thoughts and intentions.

This is by far the most challenging day of my life. Too many thoughts are coming through my mind; my intuition appears to be shutting down; or is it blocked? I can't seem to be able to connect with confidence to my Voodoo Shit anymore. Perhaps, this is a normal defence system that my intuition is undergoing. Our kids are scared, my husband is on life support, and I am alone with my thoughts. I am eagerly trying to concentrate on the tips and tools I give my clients. The only advice I have for myself is to breathe.

How ironic is that? My husband cannot breathe on his own and I am telling myself to make an effort and take a deep, cleansing breath. This will bring me peace, this will quiet my mind chatter, my negative self-talk will diminish, and it will help me to stabilize my disposition. I remain faithful to what few gut instincts are presently working for me.

I inform the boys to come back tomorrow when they are ready and to stay home from school for the next few days. Luckily, I know enough about comatose patients to know that it is encouraging to hold a twenty-four-hour vigil, read to them, play music, touch them, and speak to them, even in this state of unconsciousness. It is surprising what the subconscious mind remembers and discerns during a coma. It is highly imperative that all the above are performed daily during Tim's sleep state.

As I am fighting intense exhaustion, my father-in-law orders me to go home and sleep. He insists on staying the night with his son. How the hell do I sleep? I am uneasy leaving my husband's side as thoughts of him dying without me come flooding in.

A few days ago, even the dog sensed there was something off in our household. Animals are highly intuitive and act on organic instincts daily. Our dog, Shamus, slept by my husband's side the whole time prior to his entering the hospital. He also followed him everywhere he went throughout the house, not once leaving his side, astutely knowing that his master was desperately sick.

When I return home very late that night (or is it early in the morning the next day?), our dog looks at me with the saddest eyes. His eyes plead, asking, "Where is Tim and will he be alright?"

Patting his head, I lead him to bed for a very short night of disturbed and restless sleep. The comfort of my empty bed is not reassuring. The house feels sick.

Monday, February 11, 2013—What a Way to Spend BC Family Day

"We make up horrors to help us cope with the real ones."
Stephen King

Our two older boys are still asleep. I walk zombie-like to the kitchen to find our youngest son T.J. already eating his breakfast. He asks if he can come to the hospital with me. I explain that he can, although I need to talk to him and his brothers before they visit their dad this morning. Once the older boys are awake, we sit together on the sofa. I reach for their hands, tightly squeeze them, and hold back my tears.

I need to be strong for my boys. I am the anchor, the only lucid and available parent they have at this moment. With as few details as possible, I tell my inquisitive children that their dad now has tubes in his mouth, is unconscious, in a sleep-like state, with monitors buzzing and beeping around him all the time. We discussed this yesterday, when they said goodbye to their dad for a while.

They sit with blank looks on their faces, digesting the news. The older two decide to stay at home for a while longer. Meanwhile, T.J. and I drive to the hospital bright and early. The other boys will arrive with Jeff later on. Two other family friends arrive to show support and help out with the children during our absence. I ask one of them to flex his intuitive muscle and let me know what he feels. He softly responds, "Tim's cells are fighting and will slowly get better; it will take some time."

I sense he is holding back some information and is not entirely sharing his intuitive knowledge with me, for my own protection and sanity. I am so grateful for our friendship. Since both Tim's family and mine live further away, our circle of friends has always been our support system.

Upon arriving at the hospital, I am informed by the doctor (who has returned after only a few hours of sleep himself) that within a few hours my husband will be transferred to another hospital with more advanced resources. I panic as I have already felt part of this tiny family in the ICU ward. I know the doctor, the nurses, and the respiratory technician's (RT's) names by heart, and they know me. We have been together since our entry to the emergency ward on Saturday afternoon, two days ago. They reassured me; they took care of my husband's state and mine.

Funny how a crisis can bring total strangers close.

I do not want to have to transfer hospitals; however, they insist this is best for my husband's survival. I rush to the phone to call home and tell our two boys to get dressed quickly. They need to come and visit their dad before he leaves. I call Jeff to ask him to bring the boys as soon as possible as their dad is being transferred to another hospital within the hour. When the boys arrive at the hospital, the doctor guides us to the family room for an update. We are sitting here in a state of shock and fear dreading the worse. The doctor explains that Tim's condition is far more serious than he originally anticipated and he will be in excellent care at the other hospital, which has more resources.

I sit in silence, looking at the doctor in total disbelief. "Far more serious." The children have no expression on their faces, nor does my father-in-law, and we each have a tear rolling down our cheeks.

I force myself to breathe as it will allow my energy to flow more freely and perhaps my intuitive muscle will begin to flex more strongly. I jog my memory to continue to breathe and to not hold my breath, wishing for the spark in my gut to fully ignite. Anything? Complete and utter numbness. I am disappointed with myself.

"Get out of your head!" I scream at myself so loudly I fear others will hear me.

I am trying too hard to do something that normally comes as naturally as breathing. Again the irony of this thought sets in. I internalize a bitter laugh as my husband is no longer breathing on his own and I am holding my breath.

I call my best girlfriend, Shannon, to let her know what is happening. She is my rock and I know that I will need her strength and encouragement to get through this ordeal. We usually speak once a week and I know that she will be wondering, "Where the hell is Michèle? I haven't heard from her since…"

Through sobs, I explain what has transpired over the last days and she is in utter shock and bewilderment. She asks what she can do to help. I am so drained and exhausted that her question brings me to greater tears. She immediately senses to take charge of the conversation and decides to call key friends to start a prayer circle. Within thirty minutes, women from the United States, the local Vancouver area, and Vancouver Island gather on their phones with me as they sit silently astounded by the news and listen intently to the happenings of late. They commit to sending Tim healing, love, and light energy during this time. I dedicate Shannon as my go-to person who will inform the group and others of his progress. I ask to have our privacy respected in this day and age of social media. They happily agree. I am thankful to have spirited, empowered women in my life now. With another quick phone call to my sister in Ontario, she forms her own circle of my best buddies, the men in my life.

The ambulatory transfer team arrived when we were in the family room hearing the news from the doctor. The boys display raw emotions of sadness, fear, and helplessness. They do not like to see their dad unresponsive and lying in a bed unconscious and filled with tubes while machines buzz all around him. To distract them, the social worker intervenes and, with the help of the nurses and the transfer team, she explains what each machine does to support their dad's life.

Our middle son, Maxwell who is quite scientific is the first one to stop crying, as now he is highly interested and fascinated with the machinery. He questions the staff about every machine and wants to know more. He infers and relates how the machinery works to support his dad's life to the way an engine makes a car function. I can't help but smile for the first time in days. T.J. is too heartbroken to ask any questions as he continues to stare at his dad in disbelief. Ross our eldest pulls himself together and shows some interest. He understands his responsibilities as the oldest "man" of the house.

The ambulatory transfer team hurries along to get my husband situated in his temporary bed and geared up on the much-smaller life support machine. They assure us this is completely safe and they are in constant contact with the receiving hospital and their "home" hospital, which is St. Paul's in Vancouver. Tim is being transferred from Peace Arch Hospital in White Rock to Abbotsford Regional Hospital, approximately an hour's drive from our house. Tim was to be airlifted, yet due to the weather conditions he is transported by ground.

The new digs are fabulous! Abbotsford Regional Hospital has been recently updated and offers many resources that our much-smaller, hometown hospital cannot. The main entrance of the hospital is brightly lit with natural light coming in through the massive windows. There is a library for the bookworm, a Starbucks for the coffee connoisseur, a variety store filled with essentials, lounge chairs for comfortable seating, and a cafeteria. Is the hospital trying to make our stay inviting, I wonder? Nonetheless, I am impressed by this facility and I haven't seen the ICU ward yet.

I am dazzled by the amount of space and the sheer size of Tim's new room—yes; it is a room and a big one at that—compared to his space in the other hospital. It has a very distinct scent that I can't quite describe. It is a mix of cleaning agents, antibacterial hand soap, medications, sickness, and death. Tim's bed is much bigger and is more modern than the last. Many more machines are hooked up all around my husband here. The room has solid and real walls; the back wall is laced with windows for a perfect view of a walkway and a green space that I tell myself to discover later on. The front of the room is made up of a glass wall with matching doors in the entrance. Adjacent to the front of the room is the nurses' station. Unlike the other hospital, which only had one station for many beds, this hospital has one station per one or two beds, depending on the critical nature of the patient. Because my husband is a new resident, he is assigned his very own nurse. The staff consists of nurses, an RT, a physiotherapist, a social worker, and an intensivist doctor (one who only cares for patients in intensive care.)

The move has been hard on Tim's body and the team assures me this is completely "normal." We are not allowed into his new room until he is settled in his new bed, washed, changed, assessed by the nurses, the RT, and the intensivist. In the meantime, my father-in-law and I take advantage of touring the hospital, getting some food, going over necessary documentation, making plans for the week, and regrouping. We give each other superhero names by virtue of having been going on full speed for a few days. I am "Wonder Woman" as I have been juggling several balls at once and my father-in-law is "Batman" as he has been staying up all night with his son. We are finally allowed to come and see Tim. Dr. Blake, the intensivist checks in with us. He explains that he is well briefed from the other hospital as to which tests Tim has undergone and he will advise us when each result comes back. His plan is to have Tim on life support for a few more days until he knows what we are dealing with. We are now told that meningitis is not the cause of Tim's condition. I am relieved, although we still do not know what the cause is. One infectious disease down, so many more to rule out… What if they do not figure it out in time?

Time, what is time? In the grand scheme of things, do time and space even exist? Do we humans perceive time and space differently when we are awake, conscious, and living? Will Tim—while he is in a coma—perceive time and space the same way I do now? Each minute that goes by does not feel like sixty seconds. It feels closer to one hour. Why is time slowing down when I want it to speed up for the first time in my life? I warn myself to look at the clock no longer as it slowly, slowly ticks time away. Time is relative at this moment. Tim's body needs time to heal from the disease, the infection.

We, his family members, need time to absorb what the hell is going on! We need to take time away from our busy, hectic lives. And, time is excruciating, is cruel, and is directly laughing at me. As I glance at the clock on the wall of Tim's room, menacing visions of the clown from Stephen King's *It* movie sinisterly mock me. It is as though the clock has transformed into the clown's face. He yells out, "I have hold of time now! I am stopping the tick-tock of the clock!"

Is this my intuition playing out? How can it be? I know intuition is kind, gentle, and peaceful, although it can be firm with pressing issues. Is this my intuition being firm and wanting me to realize that this is all about time? Is this a dream, I ask myself? No! This is all very real as the clock ticks away to the next minute.

I am tired of sitting in this room already, so I decide to go and discover the walkway I saw earlier. At the back of the hospital, I also find outdoor seating and remind myself to come back and enjoy the view of the pond and the green space. This will be a good place to come back to and meditate, pray, cry, scream, punch at the air, curse at Tim, the Universe, God, and whoever else I can think of, and get in touch with my intuition as I am doing right now. Feeling my legs becoming numb from the constant sitting, I continue to walk the path as the only form of exercise I will have for a while.

My father-in-law rushes to organize for my mother-in-law and sisters-in-law to find the hospital. It is a quiet evening as I try to catch up on some sleep. I realize I can sleep better knowing Tim is on life support and I am by his side.

As I curl up on my chair with a warm blanket the nurse brought me, I hear the noise of the machines buzzing and beeping, and the green lines and numbers flashing continuously on the screens. My gut instinct reignites for a brief moment: this is what Tim was hearing and seeing days before his entry to the hospital. His intuition, his spidey senses, were preparing him for this exact day. The noise is more intense here as the room is self-contained. I hadn't noticed it before.

The nurse quietly works around my somewhat sleeping state throughout the evening, bringing my husband cooling blankets as his temperature spikes to dangerous degrees. I strain to block out the sound of the clock by focusing on the gentle hum of the ventilator as it pushes air into my husband's lungs.

The gang arrives a few hours later. Tim's mother and sister are speechless as is our sister-in-law (her lifetime partner). After filling the girls in with the details, I give them their privacy with Tim, and I am relieved to have an hour to lay my head down and try to get some rest in the designated family room. I am totally and officially out of energy. Tim's family stays a few hours; we make plans to have our sister-in-law return the next day with our boys, as my father-in-law has graciously volunteered to pick up my parents from the airport in the morning.

Since Abbotsford Regional Hospital is much further away from home, my father-in-law and I take residence in a local motel to refuel, rest as best we can, and minimize time away from Tim. My father-in-law will take the night shift and I will take the day shift, which I suspect will end closer to midnight or later. I want to return the next morning by 6:00 a.m. to allow my father-in-law proper rest and sleep. We plan on establishing a routine that is as normal as possible and we schedule frequent visits for my children. We agree the boys could come visit their dad on Tuesday rather than go to school. They will return to school on Wednesday. I do not sleep this night, new surroundings and new bed; besides I never sleep well the first night in a motel. Why would this night be different? So much is different. I am not on vacation staying in a four-star hotel. I am in a motel with the necessary amenities to get by during Tim's stay at the hospital.

I keep telling myself to sleep and rest. This is all that my husband is doing right now. He is sleeping and resting. Granted, not on purpose or because he is tired, rather, it is a necessity. Why am I not sleeping? Do I feel guilty for … for what? There is an overwhelming feeling of guilt coming upon me, but why? I lie silently in the motel bed staring at the ceiling, taking a deep breath to try and flex my intuitive muscle. It feels flabby; it feels out of shape; it feels strained. I give up, again; and subsequently fall asleep trying to avoid looking at the clock as each hour painfully passes by.

Tuesday, February 12, 2013—A Family Reunion of Sorts

"If you talk to a man in a language he understands, that goes to his head. If you talk to him in his language, that goes to his heart."
Nelson Mandela

No one prepares you for what your spouse will look like while they are on life support. It is not as we see it on television or in the movies. The actor's body does not bloat, their skin does not discolour, and their body definitely does not respond the same way as in real life.

Early in the morning, the nurse tries to stimulate my husband's toes by pressing on his nail. I wonder what will happen as Tim hates getting his toes touched. He will flinch and pull away very quickly when he is conscious. In his coma, he does not respond. I am not certain what I expected. I thought perhaps his natural instincts would have had his foot pull away briskly as he "normally" does. Yet, there is only a slight movement in his foot and the nurse is hopeful. I do not understand her hope. The nurse conducts an assessment of Tim's condition right before the change-of-shift; I did not notice the routine until a few days ago.

Earlier this morning, it was decided to stop a particular sedative and monitor Tim's reaction. This is called a "sedation vacation." Today, it'll last less than two hours. I am not certain what it accomplishes, what the results need to be, as I see no change in my husband's being. He does "cough" at times. It is peculiar how our bodies know what to do, even though we are not alert or conscious. When someone is in a coma and they cough, it appears rather painful and is quite alarming. Random body spasms also occur when a person is in a coma. This appears shocking to those who bear witness. Having experienced jerky movements and coughing, I expect to see my husband's eyes open or for him to squeeze my hand as I hold his. Such disappointment when nothing transpires. Tim is running a higher fever than the day before and the cooling blanket is not helping. A new and improved blanket is brought over that monitors his rising temperature and will adjust accordingly. Tim's heartbeat is quite irregular and the team is concerned, so an electrocardiogram (ECG) is required. This again is very common, I am told with ICU patients. They want to ensure that his heart is not being too strained during the trauma.

What about my heart? Is it not hurting, beating irregularly, and feeling the strain of the crisis, too? Along with my heart, the organ, my heart, the energetic portion is afflicted; hence, the reason for my limp intuitive muscle. The energetic heart is an integral component of our intuitive muscle. Both, the physical and energetic hearts lie at the centre of our body and spirit. They bring balance to our upper and lower bodies. I say "bodies" to refer to both the physical and energetic ones. The physical heart is a major player in allowing our body to function as it beats an average seventy-two beats per minute rhythmically circulating blood to our organs and more. Our energetic heart brings harmony and love into our life.

Am I feeling harmony and love, I ask? Tim and I had barely reconciled from our separation when he got sick. I don't believe I had truly fallen out of love with him, rather my love changed. One of the major reasons for our separation was our love had changed and faded. Tim was not loving or taking care of himself anymore; therefore, how could he love others? How could he display love if he didn't love who he was? He was not feeling the love within himself or around him. It is all in all easy to love oneself. You must display self-care routines such as engaging in your favourite pastime, eating a healthy diet, exercising or being active, doing things you enjoy just for the hell of it. Tim was no longer doing any of that. Tim was suffering from the classic case of "Not Enough Syndrome" and self-sabotage practices.

We all know it far too well, the "Not Enough Syndrome." There is not enough time, not enough money, not enough experience; I am not good enough, just not enough! It creates a block in your psyche, your beliefs about yourself, your emotional self and your overall well-being by producing feelings of inadequacy, incompetence, and insufficiency. Tim would often speak out against himself in this exact manner, leading himself to belief he was not good enough; he began to display signs of self-sabotage. He was his own worst enemy instead of his best cheerleader. Self-sabotage is when you do everything in your power to make something not happen. It produces problems in setting and achieving goals by materializing itself as procrastination, comfort eating, and an overindulgence of alcohol. You fear your own empowerment and you fear change. You become unmotivated, your dreams and inspirations are jeopardized, and your schedule may be chaotic and hectic, resulting in low productivity. I have witnessed these same dis-eases generate a blocked intuition and a downward spiral into an abyss of hell in some of my clients.

Is this the rationalization for Tim's current disease? What is the purpose of him lying in a coma, unconscious? My claircognizant tool sparks a thought—for Tim to shed this belief of himself, for Tim to become revitalized, for Tim to be gentler with himself, and for Tim to release patterns that no longer serve him. I reflect deeply on what this "time-out" in life could mean for me as well.

Today, the boys come by for a visit with their aunt and stay most of the day. They are not accustomed to seeing their dad in this comatose state, yet the new surroundings ease their discomfort. Max is thrilled to be investigating new machinery and a new room, and questions Nurse Micheline every time she enters. He wants to know what each machine is doing to assist his dad's recovery. He brings a smile to my face, as I know that he is resilient and will be strong during this time. T.J. is still quite upset and cries steadily. Max decides to cheer him up by blowing balloons with the surgical gloves. This does ease the tension and we laugh. We spend a pleasant day together, playing cards, listening to music, and playing with blown-up surgical glove-balloons.

I feel as though it is some sort of family reunion when my father-in-law arrives with my parents from Ontario in tow. As we gather and fill the ICU family room, Tim's room, and the hallway, I burst into tears as my mother holds me tightly, whispering, "We are all here now, Mich."

This does not make me feel better yet I do not have the heart to tell her. I think if Tim were to leave us, this would definitely be the optimal time. Now I feel the great sadness T.J. feels and I want to scream, "I hate this! Make it all go away! Decide to die or wake up!"

Once everyone returns home, my father-in-law takes the night shift at the hospital. Before leaving, I whisper in my husband's ear, "Don't you dare leave me until I can be here in person. I love you. Sleep well." I make a note to call the school to have the counsellors follow up with the boys. I go to our temporary home, the motel, and try to sleep.

Wednesday, February 13, 2013— Geese Talk

"Some people talk to animals. Not many listen though. That's the problem."
A.A. Milne, Winnie-the-Pooh

Apparently overnight, Tim had an allergic reaction to one of his many antibiotics. His stats went through the roof. He demonstrated increased stress on his heartbeat and other vital signs. So it was necessary to place him back on the drug propofol. Everyone including the staff is required to wear gloves, masks, and gowns. Since we are not certain what we are dealing with, it is for our protection and Tim's. Dr. Blake performs a bronchoscopy to inspect the lungs and retrieve a specimen. We know from the X-rays that Tim's lungs are both infected internally and on the outer walls of the lungs. Dr. Blake informs us it could be a fungal or a viral pneumonia. Tim's fever continues to rise, his body continues to swell, he is still heavily sedated, and he is displaying no improvement.

I am hoping for good news today, since the doctor at Peace Arch had indicated Tim would be only a few days on life support. There is still no change, no news, and no confirmation as to what the heck is afflicting my husband. Much speculation… The doctor had informed me that the longer a patient is on life support, the greater the chances of developing pneumonia, which my husband is currently afflicted with or other side effects.

Feeling terribly exasperated by sitting in this room, having little to no sleep, and seeing no change, I decide to take a longer walk than normal. It is a cloudy day with a warm breeze.

As I walk the path, I notice two Canada geese on the grass. The one is looking at me intensely; as I walk to the left, he turns his head left; as I walk to the right, he turns his head right. I stop, he approaches. We display a natural curiosity for one another. The other goose is sitting in the grass also staring at me with great intensity. Being in touch with nature and loving the animal kingdom, I know they are trying to relay a message to me. I slow my pace and then I am prompted to look up to the roof of the hospital where there sit at least twenty Canada geese, all of them looking at me as I walk. The goose sitting on the grass starts to honk intently and persistently as I walk by. When I stop walking with my back to the goose, she stops honking. I turn around to look at her and she honks again.

I close my eyes, focus on my breath, and the first thought is that I must keep my strength and courage up for Tim as he is doing the same. With my clairaudient tool functioning, I hear, "No goose ever dies alone."

I begin to cry as they, the geese, are telling me Tim will not be alone if and when he dies. I thank them for the greeting and the words of encouragement, and I continue walking the path that leads back to the entrance of the hospital. Upon returning to Tim's room, I text my friend who is my Reiki teacher and a shaman asking her to look up the meaning of the goose spirit and to send Tim some healing Reiki energy. That night, I sleep through the night for the first time in many days.

Thursday, February 14, 2013— Valentine's Day

"A healer's power stems not from any special ability, but from maintaining the courage and awareness to embody and express the universal healing power that every human being naturally possesses."
Eric Micha'el Leventhal

I have been playing music and reading out loud each day since Tim's coma was induced. Today is no different. I decide to flip through my collection and I choose The Eagles singing "Hotel California," one of Tim's favourites. As I listen to the music, I picture Tim and myself dancing together. We have never been to Hotel California in Baja, Mexico and I imagine us dancing in its lobby feeling the soft warm wind flowing through the open doors. His nurse today is Dallas, who has been enjoying the music too. He reassures me it is very soothing for Tim. It creates an environment of peace and calm. I notice Dallas busting a move every now and again to the English band Tears for Fears. It brightens my day.

I have also decided to write about our experience, my feelings, reactions from others, make a list of the hospital routines, and list the many, many medications Tim receives. I have set up a space on the counter to the left of Tim's bed where I am placing mementos he receives. The space is filled with get-well cards, crystals that I have brought in to help clear the energies of the room, and Valentine's Day balloons. Images of angels and saints and positive affirmations brought in by other family members adorn the space as well.

My father-in-law surprises me one day, arriving in hand with a little angel figurine that he has had at his house. It sat by the phone for years collecting dust and seemed forgotten. It was handmade for him by the father of his good friend who told my father-in-law it was his guardian angel. One day, having to go back home and check on things, he noticed the figurine. He instinctively picked it up and brought it with him to the hospital. This gesture warmed my heart. I am reserved and reluctant to share my beliefs on intuition and all of this Voodoo Shit with my father-in-law, as he is such a pragmatic man. I guess it will be too late now to hide my secret identity from him, especially if he decides to read this book.

My phone tweets the familiar sound of an incoming text. It is from my Reiki teacher, Lynne. The message is so profound and accurate from what I heard the day before from the geese. It reads, "Goose goes the distance and shows the way in turbulent times. They are both leaders and followers. If a goose is sick or injured, another goose will always remain at its side until it gets well. No goose ever dies alone."

Lynne tried to send Tim Reiki upon receiving my request yesterday; however, she was unable to do so. She indicates that Tim's soul did not give her permission. When I ask why, she says that she feels a big bubble around him that she cannot penetrate and it seems as though he is making a decision. She soothes my worrisome thoughts by adding, she will try again to see if the bubble changes. I break down in tears and share this text message with the night nurse, Micheline.

Micheline and I have grown a special bond as I have with each nurse that tends to Tim. Her husband is a highly intuitive man who believes and has experienced many of the things that I do. She, on the other hand, has not been able to connect to her intuition as easily yet always finds it fascinating. We have shared stories, laughed, and even cried a bit together. Micheline shares with me that the geese have been at the hospital since its renovations and have never left. She is not surprised by the message of goose spirit and it makes sense to her.

I tell Micheline a certain song keeps running through my mind. She knows I play music each day and asks if it is from my playlist. I answer no. Rather it is "Die Young," with the following lyrics repeating themselves, "I can hear your heartbeat …" and "… like we're going to die young." I remember hearing it on the radio the day Tim was transferred to Abbotsford.

I am feeling quite overwhelmed with guilt and shame today, after receiving the message from goose spirit and from constantly hearing the song "Die Young" replaying in my head. Allow me to explain my guilt. For starters, in the past while creating our wills, Tim discussed with me that he never wanted to be on life support, lifeless, and in a comatose state. He wanted to remain in control of his bodily functions and insisted I never allow him to be helpless, hooked to a machine, as he is today. He had instructed me to "pull the plug." Am I going against his wishes by allowing him to lie there still and silent in the hospital bed?

I plan out his funeral or is it a Celebration of Life he wanted? Why can't I recall the details? My powers of observation and attention to details are typically in high gear. Did Tim want us to wear yellow at his Celebration of Life, his favourite colour? Or, did he want to have a funeral, dressed as Dracula and the guests arrive in costumes in honour of his favourite holiday, Halloween?

I am torn as to what to do if the day comes when he dies. I do not want to make the wrong decision. Am I doing him a disservice by not "pulling the plug," since he is in the exact state he did not want to be in? I struggle with these questions and more for hours on end as I stare blankly at my husband's lifeless body. I certainly hope he will not be disappointed with me, if and when he survives. Will he ever forgive me, if and when he wakes up? Will he haunt me forever if he dies? This is a whole other topic… Again, I am filled with guilt and shame, as I am not respecting his wishes. On the other hand, the doctor (how many days ago was that?) did inform my incoherent husband he'd be intubated. Did Tim even understand what it meant at the time? If only for a brief second, I tell myself he did understand.

Secondly, I feel as though I should have paid more attention to my husband during his first few days of being sick. I should have intuited more intently the "warning signs" of what Tim was hearing and seeing—the numbers, the buzzing, and the lines—specifically in colour. Having just recently gotten back together from our separation, I was not entirely overjoyed.

Lastly, the knowing, the feeling from the first that Tim would die young! How does one deal with that? It is not every day a person has such knowing of another's looming death like I have done. I have had foreknowledge, foresight, and premonitions of people's deaths many times before and they have all manifested. A curse or a gift, I ask you? The jury is still out in my mind.

During the turbulent times in our marriage, I would often think, "Wouldn't it be easier if Tim would just die, so I didn't have to ask for a separation?" There would be no "bad" guy feeling. Or would there? This is the ultimate source of my guilt. That exact thought right there! Forget the fact that I intuitively received this message over and over again, since that beautiful, magical day of our wedding back in 1992. There would be no one to blame if he died. Well, guess again. I am the one to blame and I feel the shame. I did not precisely wish for my husband's death. I simply hoped that it could manifest before I needed to be the one to initiate the separation with our dissolving marriage. So when it did not, the thought went away temporarily because we had experienced an emotional death— the separation. I have only shared this awareness of mine with a few trusted confidants and I would always get very upset with them when they felt our separation was the source of the death I intuitively saw and heard.

Standing looking out to the crisp blue sky one early morning in January, I had again heard, "Once Tim is happy again, he will suffer another death."

"Holy shit, GOD! What the 'F' is going on? Do not start this again!" I thought and yelled back to God. This is *a load of crock*. Who the hell does He think He is? I began to really question this figure of God that we pray to and worship. I was beginning to feel as though this perception of God is not what we think He is. How can God *dangle this rabbit* in front of my face again and I hear His laughter? Would the peaceful, righteous God laugh out loud in my face? I think not! I don't have time to reflect on this whole image of who we really think God is, yet I have a strong suspicion He is wearing a mask and is disguised as someone else…

The major problem with intuitive messages, especially pictures, images, and symbols, are that they can have a figurative meaning. It is at times difficult to see past what you already perceive the image or the symbol to actually mean. I already know this. So when I initially received the message of Tim's death, it came as words that I heard through my clairaudient tool. There was no image. The images and symbols came much later. I recommend to my clients when your intuitive thought is confusing or difficult to understand, ask for clarity. I did the same. I asked for more information, for a clearer understanding of what Tim's death would mean—emotional or physical. Each time I asked, I received the same answer, an overall death, no more, no less. This did not suffice, as it did not give me more facts. I was getting worn out. So, how could I have misinterpreted this meaning for so long? Beats the shit out of me. All I know for sure is my husband is lying on his deathbed at this moment in time. Was I wrong all those years to think it would be a physical death? No, I wasn't! In speaking to those few friends who always suggested an emotional death, they were quite alarmed and silenced at this point upon hearing the dreaded news.

I contemplate the clairaudience I received in January when I heard that Tim would die again when he felt happy to be reunited with me, and I tell myself Tim is in fact dying of sorts. He is releasing old beliefs and patterns that serve him no longer. When he pulls through and is removed from life support, he'll be a different man. He will recognize his own superpowers, his own "spidey-senses," and flex his intuitive muscle like he has never done before. He will experience gratitude, a greater sense of being, and discover his passions. His personal outlook of himself will be reignited. He will display confidence, strength, and care for himself.

I realize that it is up to him, not me anymore. It is his business, not mine. I never thought that I had "pushed" my beliefs on Tim. Yet, sitting watching my husband's lifeless, unconscious body, I realize I have not been satisfied with him for quite some time. I witnessed him falling into a rut, a downward spiral, and going to the dark side so many times. Why could he not just move past it? I did, so long ago. I evolved; I changed. I would have thought after all these years of being together that he would naturally rise above with me. I have come to the conclusion today that this is his journey, not mine. His death—whatever form it will take—needs to happen for him. So, I sit by his side, watch and wait.

LEGIONNAIRES' DISEASE?

Tim's condition is slowly improving as the day progresses. His temperature finally stabilizes at 37.5°, his heart rate stays at 93 beats per minute, his oxygen level has been turned down to 50 percent, and his oxygen intake is steady and his body is trying to initiate breathing on its own.

Dr. Blake informs me that he called Public Health yesterday and the infectious disease nurse came in today to assess Tim. Obviously, this is much more serious than originally thought.

I question the good doctor as to why he would notify Public Health. He suspects Legionnaires' disease and should have the results confirmed by tomorrow. He strongly advises me not to Google the disease. I recall hearing about some outbreak in the United States. We chat briefly regarding the next steps.

Dr. Blake has administered the necessary antibiotics to fight off the disease and is confident Tim will pull through due to his age and overall health. When my father-in-law arrives for his shift, the doctor is gone, and I debrief him on the news. My father-in-law gives me more information regarding the disease. Legionnaires' is not a common disease and less than one hundred people are diagnosed in Canada a year. Most people infected with the disease may not even have been tested for it; therefore, I am extremely grateful for Dr. Blake's suspicions.

Legionella are vicious bacteria that live in water or soil and result in Legionnaires' disease in humans. It affects the respiratory glands and develops into very serious pneumonia. The name originates from the outbreak, which occurred in Philadelphia in 1976 and killed twenty-nine Legionnaires who had attended an American Legion Convention. The hotel's cooling tower was infected with *Legionella* bacteria, which spread through the air conditioning system. It is most often found and linked to wet sources and environments usually in warmer waters where algae and organic matter are present. It is often found in hotels, cruise ships, whirlpool spas, hot tubs, showerheads, and humidifiers.

Many of the symptoms of Legionnaires' disease will first appear as flu-like, and then progress to high fever, chills, dry cough, chest pain, confusion, hallucinations, kidney failure, and septic shock. Tim exhibited most of these. It can be treated and most patients will survive the disease with antibiotics and hospitalization if it is properly detected through a series of tests that may include but are not limited to examining lung tissue, blood, and sputum samples. I feel a bit hopeful, because we think we know what we are dealing with.

My dear friend Marina comes by to visit this evening. She comes adorned with balloons, bags filled with food, and essential oils for Tim's healing. I am so grateful for her beautiful, uplifting smile and demeanour. Marina and I give Tim some Reiki as we stand by his left and right sides. Marina surrounds Tim with her intentions, filled with symbols of roses and infinity signs. She pictures him cradled in God's hand while she calls upon the elements of water, wind, earth, and fire to expedite his healing. She notices that his head is facing north, which is the position for rejuvenation. Most of the rooms in ICU have the patients' heads facing north. I wonder if the hospital rooms were built this way on purpose or is it just a fluke? Marina indicates that Tim is strong, is fighting, is floating there, and watching to see how much I love him. This is the first time Marina has met my husband and she tells me his greenish-blue eyes are bright; incidentally, his eyes are green. His eyes have been closed throughout his coma. She asks me what TV show he likes to watch with me and I reply, "*Grey's Anatomy.*"

She states we are living an episode of *Grey's Anatomy.*

Friday, February 15, 2013—Reiki, Sidekicks, and More

"The way we get into these scrapes and get out of them, it's almost as though someone was dreaming up these situations; guiding our destiny."
Robin to Batman

I have barely slept this past night. I have been staring at the clock since 3:00 a.m. *Getting up is for the dogs*. After tossing and turning for more than two hours, I get ready to return to the hospital. I briefly think Tim is lucky to be sleeping for the better part of six days, despite my lack of it. Anger fills me, as I am envious of him being able to sleep undisturbed, even if it is an induced sleep. When I arrive at 6:00 a.m., Tim's temperature is wavering around his normal at 36.9°. It tends to elevate a bit during the evening hours. For the most part, it will stay between 36.9° and 38.6° all day. I am pleased to see his oxygen set at 45 percent by mid-afternoon and his heart rate is in the low nineties for most of today. I try giving Tim Reiki, since Tim's soul did not give Lynne permission for healing through distance Reiki. I am glad that his spirit is welcoming and receiving Reiki from me. I concentrate on his infected lung with raccoon spirit to tear apart the disease.

ॐ Raccoon is My Power Animal

Raccoon spirit is my power animal and she presents herself often during Reiki treatments. The word "raccoon" originates from the Algonquin Indian word "arckunem" meaning "hand scratcher." Raccoons by nature are very dexterous and full of disguise. They like to use their paws in various ways to open things and are very meticulous in washing their food in water prior to eating, especially veggies and fruits. They adapt well to changes in their environment as we humans encroach on their natural habitats. Most importantly, they are masters of disguise. We all recognize raccoons by the striking masks they wear. Masks have been worn over time and for centuries during ceremonies, celebrations, performances, and even during mystical practices. They are symbols in theatre where people transform themselves into others. It didn't surprise me to find out that raccoon is my power animal. I can relate to so many of the assets and characteristics of this animal.

Your animal spirit has been with you your whole life and wants to be "unearthed," so it can help guide you through your life in making decisions, confronting challenging times, and setting goals.

I reminisce about the day I discovered my power animal is raccoon. It was during a deep meditation with a partner on a very sunny day. My partner suggested that I take her black glove and place it over my eyes to create a darker environment for my meditation. After the meditation and upon "unmasking" raccoon as my power animal, my partner and I broke out into laughter. Every participant in the room looked our way and wondered what was so funny, because the experience of finding one's power animal is quite profound.

Just picture, if you will, a black glove covering my eyes just as the eyes of the raccoon are laced in a black strip of fur. Even before the meditation began, raccoon had made her way through in spirit, claiming herself to me and exposing herself to my partner. Subsequently, raccoon spirit has been my sidekick during Reiki treatments.

Every great superhero has a sidekick. Batman has Robin, Lone Ranger has Tonto, Buffy the Vampire Slayer has Willow, Harry Potter has Hermione and Ron, Luke Skywalker has

Chewbacca, and so on. Aren't you curious to find out which animal spirit is your sidekick? If so, please refer to contact details at the end of the book to schedule your next meditation with me and we can discover your sidekick.

Dr. Blake arrives to speak to me and gives me the scoop on Tim's condition. It is in fact Legionnaires' disease, which he has suspected since our arrival on Monday, February 11. I ask him how he suspected it was this particular disease. He chuckles shyly and responds, "It was the odour emanating from your husband."

I tell the doctor I smelled it too, back on Friday, February 8 when I arrived home from work wondering if it was the smell of death. I am glad to hear that Dr. Blake has a fine "spidey-sense" of smell, clairscence, as he detected my husband's illness through his intuitive muscle. He states he has only smelled it once before, five years ago when he treated another patient with Legionnaires'. I wonder if he smells other diseases; I never get the chance to ask him.

This could be a good time for me to tell Dr. Blake he possesses this tool; unfortunately, he is very busy today and quickly inquires if I stayed away from the Internet last night. I reply that I did; however, my father-in-law gave me some basic information about the disease. He confidently informs me Tim does not fit the typical category of other patients since he is a non-smoker, not a heavy drinker, and is young. Dr. Blake notifies me that Tim would have had prolonged exposure to the bacteria and questions if anyone else in the family is displaying similar symptoms. I answer no. He assures me it is not contagious and there is no way of testing to see if we have been exposed. He had purposely not told me of his suspicions and had already started the necessary treatments for the Legionnaires'; he was just waiting for confirmation prior to discussing it with me.

Dr. Blake hands me a package about the disease that I am welcome to review anytime, as I do with some of the other documents that come across the nurse's station. Sadly, his X-ray results have not changed yet and it will take some time for the disease to disappear from his lungs. It will be a lengthy recovery and Tim will be on antibiotics for at least three weeks or longer after his release from the hospital. I am pleased for a diagnosis and the doctor assures me that Tim should be fine.

This morning, as I arrived at the hospital, I was greeted with a "Good morning" as two geese flew by and honked. I did not see the geese yesterday and I wondered where they were. It is very foggy with the sun just barely poking through the clouds. It reminds me of the "Light at the end of the tunnel." I have a feeling today will be a good day in Tim's progress.

There is a certain routine for the patients in ICU. In the morning, Tim gets his teeth brushed with a disposable brush loaded with a mouthwash-toothpaste mixture. I laugh to myself as I notice the nurse do this, as Tim hated the taste of the mixture when he was at Peace Arch Hospital. At least, he is in a coma and doesn't know. His temperature is checked, eye drops are administered to avoid dry eyes, all IV lines and tubes are checked, his reaction to pain is checked by pressing on a toenail, he is repositioned, and more.

Each nurse speaks to Tim as though he is wide-awake by greeting him and telling him what the procedure is going to be for the morning. Everything the nurse does, he lets Tim know. The night-time routine is similar and includes a bath as it helps to calm the patient. The nurses know the importance of communicating with ICU patients and are very considerate. Nurse Dallas informs me that Tim's arterial line will need to be removed today, since it has been malfunctioning overnight. Apparently, they are only good for so many days before needing to be replaced.

Despite Tim having many visitors, I am feeling alone and lonely. As the day develops, the sun grows brighter and the weather is warmer outside. I take advantage of this sudden change in the weather for February and stroll my walkway more often today.

I reflect on last night's dream. Our wonderful Uncle Jim who passed away many years ago came for a visit. He explained that Tim is wondering if he should stay or go. I respond to Uncle Jim that it isn't up to me yet it would be nice if Tim decided to stay. I feel better thinking back to my dream and my hope is restored with caution. The sun kisses my cheeks as I feel the warmth. I should be happier…

After morning rounds, Dr. Blake informs me that Tim's sedation will be turned off and another ECG will be administered. Now, we wait…

The last time Tim's sedation was turned off; there was absolutely no change, no reaction, and lots of disappointment. I did not know what to expect—a sudden miracle where Tim would wake up and say "Hi." I was emotionally, physically, and spiritually drained that day, despite the doctor telling me that there might be no response.

Today, I know what to expect during this second sedation vacation—nothing. I have no expectations; therefore, there will no disappointments. The medical team is looking for the slightest response from physical movements to the stats regulating. Four and a half hours later, there is no response from Tim—again. His fever rose and his oxygen level needed to be adjusted many times. This is the longest vacation he has had and the nurse states Tim reacted just fine and this is good news. The last time he was on vacation, his stats could not handle the effects of the reduction in sedation, and after one hour or so he needed to be returned to full sedation. I do not feel as excited as the nurse.

My father-in-law is a great help with organizing Tim's benefit package with his employer to take care of some finances. In the meantime, I sit by, watch Tim, and wonder if this feeling of hope is real. Am I filled with hope because he will wake up or will I have to make a life-changing decision? No one seems to want to have the discussion about whether Tim dies and I am rightfully pissed! I have tried in the gentlest ways to approach the subject with no response back. Everyone is probably scared for me and does not want to upset me further. What they do not know is that avoiding this subject is making me angrier than seeing my husband in a damn coma! Even my mom doesn't talk about it. The most excruciating part of this is I speak to no one about these feelings and thoughts that are present. I hold it all in and suffer in silence.

Saturday, February 16, 2013—An Emotional Roller Coaster Ride

"The boundaries which divide Life from Death are at best shadowy and vague. Who shall say where the one ends, and where the other begins?"
Edgar Allan Poe

Many negative test results came back yesterday and today. Karishma, the RT, turns down the ventilator in the hope that Tim will breathe more on his own. Healthy people typically breathe about twelve breaths a minute, whereas Tim's breathing is over-compensated and he is taking twenty to thirty per minute, Karishma clarifies. This is not unusual for sick patients and it explains why his heart rate gets too elevated, and then the ventilator is turned back to 100 percent. Karishma explains that Tim's breaths are not like hers or mine, since the machine offers support in terms of oxygen and PEEP (positive-end expiratory pressure) levels. PEEP levels are optimized to assist the lungs to expand and collapse, to regulate the alveoli pressure. In essence, the ventilator is doing all this for Tim; he is simply carrying on from the jump-start of the machine. Two hours later, Karishma is satisfied with Tim's results and the progress so far. Then, she notices his system becoming too stressed; therefore, she places the ventilator back to full capacity. Since his temperature has risen to higher levels, she instructs the nurse to place the cooling blanket back on Tim.

I met with the Infectious Diseases Control doctor yesterday. He confirms Legionnaires' and informs us that we can remove our hospital gowns. Now that we know the only disease Tim has is Legionnaires', the doctor is confident that masks and gloves will suffice. He explains to me that the recovery process will be lengthy, as Dr. Blake had stated earlier. He informs the medical team that some of the medication given to Tim can be weaned off or removed completely. I am told this should help during the next sedation vacation as many of the medications have side effects of drowsiness. Does that even make a difference when a patient is in a coma? I am told it does, since it is a medically induced coma. Yet, I still wonder if it is possible for a patient to go into his own coma, despite it originally being induced medically? I do not see the doctors again today, so I cannot ask.

I am experiencing so many emotions throughout this critical event—some slight happiness, then extreme sorrow, not to mention profound rage—all within what feels like a few short minutes. I am trying so hard to keep my mask on, the mask of optimism. Being positive is draining me; for once in my life, why can't I be negative? I do not want to smile the fake smile anymore. I do not want to pretend that everything will be all right, like everyone tells me. I am sick and tired of hearing this bloody sentence. How do we know everything will be just fine? It seems as though everyone is ignoring the fact that my husband, my children's father, might actually die. Or is it denial? Are we pretending death does not exist? Is this why no one wants to discuss with me the cruel reality that he might die? Are they trying to remain positive? There are a multitude of opposites *floating in the air*. I am reminded for every positive there is a negative. Yin and yang, male and female, black and white, anti-matter and matter. Emotions in the form of hope and despair, joy and sadness.

Today is day seven. Three days have already gone by since the original timeframe of keeping Tim on life-support. His lungs are acutely infected with Legionnaires'; will they become more damaged or susceptible to another pneumonia? Are there increased risks involved in keeping him in a coma for longer?

Could there be further complications? Will Tim exhibit brain damage or will other organs be affected by the lack of proper oxygen flow? Will this lengthy process be a failure as the machine meant to save his life can very well be making it worse?

The doctor and his medical team have already tried waking Tim up three times without success. I am discouraged and I do not ask these questions, probably because I don't want to know the answers.

My father-in-law decided yesterday to go back home soon and organize a few things on his home front. He will return with my mother-in-law who had to go home mid-week. It was too difficult for her to see her son in such a state each day. My father is scheduled to leave for his home in Ontario after the weekend and my mother will stay on for at least another week. Our children have gone back to school and their after-school activities to help instill a sense of normalcy. They have visited every other day since we arrived in Abbotsford. I still have not returned home. I will go home tonight.

Before I leave Tim's hospital room, I whisper sternly in his ear so his dad can't hear, "You'd better not die while I am away!"

As I drive home, my mood changes and lifts somewhat. I am looking forward to seeing our boys and our dog. I feel a meagre sign of glee, then instant disgrace. I cuss and scream. I am furious, as I want to get off this emotional roller coaster ride. I crank up the radio, sing along to the song, "Die Young," which happens to be the song playing on the FM station and focus solely on driving home safely.

Sunday, February 17, 2013—*Lights, Action, and Camera*

"Do not dwell in the past, do not dream of the future, concentrate the mind on the present moment."
Buddha

I arrive at the hospital at 8:30 a.m. I do my regular routine of setting my jacket and bags on the hanger and floor outside Tim's room. I sanitize my hands. I place my gloves and mask on. I see Tim through the nurse's window; he is "sleeping" as always. My father-in-law is not in the family room, so I figure he is at the cafeteria. I greet the day nurse, Erica. As always, I walk into Tim's room and I cheerfully announce, "Good morning Tim, I'm here."

Every other day, Tim lies there, unresponsive. Today, he opens his eyes when I speak! I quickly walk over to him, take his hand in mine, and whisper, "I love you."

He tries saying it back. It is impossible to talk with so many tubes jammed down his throat. His eyes begin to tear up and I see that he is very frightened. I reassure my husband that I will be with him all day and I will be by his side most of the night.

My father-in-law arrives at this point declaring that Sue, the night nurse, was able to have Tim open his eyes on command around 4:00 a.m. I am thrilled to hear this. After I left last night, Tim had gently squeezed his sister and sister-in-law's hands. I feel like a parent who has missed her baby's first steps! I remind myself to regulate my emotions as Tim is not in the clear yet. I do not want to tire Tim out too much, as I am sure this is a huge undertaking for him. He does squeeze my hand weakly and moves his foot when I ask.

When Erica asks Tim if he is experiencing pain, he responds with a slight head movement of yes. She answers that she will give him some medication and Tim quickly tries shaking his head no, causing his heart rate to rise. Erica wants him to calm down and gently reminds him he is in the hospital and she is taking good care of him. Throughout the day, Tim yawns while determined to fight the urge to sleep. I must continually remind him I am here so he must rest. I hold his hand as I have done every day since our arrival at the hospital back on February 9. I sense he needs this reassurance more than ever. I can tell he is very confused and scared. The music is still softly playing in the background as the sun shines through the window creating a serene and peaceful environment. I give him more Reiki in the hopes of soothing Tim's emotions as he begins to cry; again, a difficult task with tubes down his throat.

The medical team does not feel confident enough to reduce Tim's medications any more, as they can tell he is displaying the onset of ICU delirium by late afternoon. His oxygen levels are still quite high and his temperature has also risen close to 40°. It is imperative for Tim to remain calm and at ease. How does one do this when they are filled with tubes, don't know where they are, don't know why they are there, and are relatively conscious?

The boys come by the hospital to see their dad and are very happy to hear he is showing some signs of responsiveness. T.J. is ecstatic to see his dad's green eyes again. Maxwell is a bit more cautious as he understands his dad still has a long way to go medically. Ross is very emotional and states he'd rather see his dad in a coma than struggling and suffering in pain. Many emotions are flowing freely throughout Tim's room. I can appreciate how the other families in the ICU ward have been feeling too. Over the course of eight days, I have witnessed two sets of families come and go as their relative has pulled through life support. They wished us the best of luck and gave us words of encouragement as they left the ICU ward. I felt jealous and envious of them during those moments, longing for our day when we could leave. Additionally, I know a family down the hall was not so fortunate. I greedily hoped the grim reaper would avoid Tim.

Monday, February 18, 2013—Much Disappointment

"Your intuition knows what to do. The trick is getting your head to shut up so you can hear."
Louise Smith

Yesterday was an exhausting day for everyone, including Tim. He did not sleep much throughout the day nor at night-time.

Today I arrive extra early around 6:00 a.m. Tim is already wide-awake despite some sedation and his hands are tied to the bed. Sue is his nurse again and informs me Tim slept less than three hours. She cautions us that today may be a difficult day for him, because of the lack of sleep, and besides Tim is not listening well. I ask him why he didn't want to fall asleep knowing that he cannot answer me by speaking out loud. I intuit that he is frightened and he no longer wants to venture to the dark side.

When I question if this is so, he nods his head yes. I reassure him not to be fearful; I am here. I do not know what his near-death experience has been or where he has been. Questioning the nurse as to why he is tied down, she informs me that my dear husband was trying to pull out his tubes overnight. I cannot imagine what it feels like to have tubes down my throat and be conscious.

I decide to read to him to keep his mind off the tubes and the fact his hands are tied. I have been reading *The Four Agreements* by Miguel Ángel Ruiz. Tim seems to be distracted by the soothing sound of my voice and dozes off as I read. I head off for a walk outside as Tim continues to rest. I notice two Canada geese sitting on the rooftop right by his room. The message I hear today is "It will not be long now." I know it means Tim will be out of ICU soon. I so badly want to fully trust my intuition and the message from goose spirit. Yet I am leery, with reason.

Tim and I develop a system of communication to show discomfort, which involves pointing to different parts of his body and a series of nods and shakes of the head. Tim is also constantly pointing out the door, as he wants to leave the hospital and this room. I tell him this is not possible for now. I have never seen a grown man so disappointed in my entire life with such an answer. It breaks my heart and I ask Tim to refrain from pointing out the door as it is too upsetting for both of us.

I was quite distraught and emotional last night, much like Ross was, because I felt so helpless. There is nothing I can physically do to help Tim more than what I am already doing by standing at his side. I know he is trying to ask for ice or a drink and he cannot have that. It is impossible and dangerous to drink with feeding and air tubes down one's throat. Tim is crushed by this news. Christine, his nurse today, tells me it is not unusual for life-support patients to be extremely thirsty when they begin to come out of the coma and wake up. I refrain from drinking in front of Tim.

My father-in-law has purchased a small dry-erasable board in the hopes of communicating with Tim. This is getting him too agitated, as his demands are not being met. One of the first words Tim tries to get us to spell out is "Hell." My father-in-law and I both know Tim means "Hell"; however; we quickly change it to "Ice," knowing he had asked for it earlier. I have a feeling Tim is trying to tell us he has been to "Hell" and this intuitively feels right to me. I make a mental note to ask him if this is so, much, much later, after his recovery.

Most of Tim's sedatives are turned off as much as they can be; for now; they will be off for approximately two hours. The ventilator, which provides oxygen levels and PEEP levels, is still turned on and the RT has been adjusting the levels throughout the two hours. The medical team places Tim back on full life-support with more sedation as his heart rate is increasing, as are his other stats. I am glad to hear Tim remembers he is in the hospital and he wants to know why. I tell him that he has a severe pneumonia. There is no point trying to explain Legionnaires' disease when I am the only one talking at the moment, plus I can still clearly see the fear building up in his eyes. Later on, Tim is pointing to his tubes and I presume he wants them taken out. He nods with a resounding yes. Once again, more disappointment!

I stay with Tim until almost one in the morning. His dad stays overnight, as he has been doing each night. Tim is not happy to see me go. I promise to see him closer to regular waking morning hours and I plead with him to fall asleep tonight. His eyes fill with tears and horror as I leave, crying myself. I collapse on the motel bed and cry some more. It is strenuous to dishearten my husband. We all get let down in our lifetimes. We begin to hear "No" or "You can't," said by our parents who think they are protecting us as children or maybe just because.... We set up expectations for others and ourselves as adults, which lead to disappointment.

Throughout the several days of Tim's coma, I have contemplated what I could be doing differently in our relationship once he wakes up. I come to the conclusion one of the tendencies I have is to say "No" to Tim more times than he cares to hear. I also realize we both set expectations we can't always fulfill, hence leading to dissatisfaction. Making a promise to myself to reduce my answer of "no" and to erase the expectations from our relationship, I feel as though I have already failed. How many times have I said "No" to Tim in a span of approximately twenty hours today? I lost count.

Tuesday, February 19, 2013—Finally, A Yes

"Intuition is seeing with the soul."
Dean Koontz

Just as the events of February 9 happened quickly when Tim was first brought to the ER and then induced into a coma, today's events also happen very quickly. I woke up this morning thinking this must all be a dream. How can it be ten days since Tim was induced in a medical coma? My, our life is so different now and will continue to be.

Once more, I am told Tim did not sleep much overnight and is experiencing greater symptoms of ICU delirium. His heart rate continues to escalate and his breathing is very laboured. It seems that yesterday's progress is not even apparent today. He is sleeping as I arrive shortly after 6:00 a.m. I am quiet, so as to not disturb his rest. Tim can feel my presence with his clairsentient tool and opens his eyes. I urge him to continue to rest so he can heal and get stronger. He so badly wants to leave the hospital and doesn't recall why he needs to be here. I refresh his memory and insist he rest for a while. He communicates as best he can that he did not want to fall asleep because I was not with him. I promise to stay later this evening or until he falls asleep. I place my name on the board and instruct Tim to point to the board if he wants me when I am not here.

Christine is his nurse and River is his RT. Together, they have an aggressive plan to have Tim breathing on his own today with oxygen support and removing the ventilator. I am impressed by their plan, yet I am keeping my emotions in check. I am done with this ride. The doctor is equally confident that Tim is almost ready to have the life-support system removed. The team is present most of the day buzzing around the room. They are adjusting medications, oxygen, PEEP levels, and intakes, hoping to have Tim lift his head up, stabilize his breaths under forty breaths per minute, reduce oxygen pressure support, and cough on his own. Christine's goal is to have Tim's stress and anxiety levels decreased so they can attempt to remove the tubes.

I am uneasy thinking what if the tubes come out and Tim needs to be reintubated. Has this ever happened before? I must ask the doctor when I see him next. Around 12:30 p.m., the medical team is feeling confident the time has arrived to remove the tubes. Christine and River give Tim instructions prior to removing the life-support machine. It is imperative he understands the instructions before pulling out the equipment. I stand by and offer support, keeping my hands on his knee. Tim is asked to cough as hard as he can so they can remove the ventilator without damaging his lungs, his airway, and his stomach (from the feeding tube). Within seconds, all tubes have been removed from Tim's mouth. He tries to muster a smile and mouths, "Hello, I love you."

We feel as though we are on *ninth cloud*, our love for one another having been brought to life as Tim has been. Thoughts of loving a prince charming are easy; loving a man with his challenges is more difficult. I reciprocate the greeting and caution him to not speak. There will be plenty of time to speak later. For now, let's concentrate on building his strength and waiting for the next steps in his recovery. Tim is still quite perplexed and unnerved. We sit in silence for most of the afternoon, trying to catch up on sleep. In the late afternoon, Tim's central IV line is removed. Tim is asking for water and a drink. His nurse informs him that he must wait at least six hours after having the ventilator removed before drinking anything. The time is required to build up the muscle strength for swallowing.

Again, more deafening nos! Soon, I tell Tim, I can't bear to speak another no.

Everyone is thrilled to see Tim no longer on the ventilator. He is wearing an oxygen mask, as he still needs the help. The children are happy to see their dad more alert and responsive. We spend a quiet evening as a family in the comfort of Tim's hospital room, watching him savour the melting ice chip on his tongue. A few hours later, he is given his first glass of water in over ten days. We can see the gratitude flood Tim's eyes as tears build. For me, I feel as though I am a first-time parent again as I watch Tim cautiously sip the water. He is quite proud of himself. In no time at all, he will be able to drink some juice, his nurse tells us. Tim attempts a "high five." We laugh together. It feels nice to hear genuine laughter filling the room. The boys' eyes are gleaming with delight and my mother expresses thankfulness. After the children and my mother leave, I stay with Tim until he falls peacefully asleep. Despite this joyous occasion, I prompt myself that he is not totally *out of the forest*.

Wednesday, February 20, 2013—We Are Moving

"It is through science that we prove, but through intuition that we discover."
Henri Poincare

I am pleased to hear Tim slept better this evening and only asked for his father once throughout the night. Tim will be moved to a High Acuity Unit today since he is progressing nicely. It is amazing how quickly he seems to be recovering. Tim's strength is slowly building up with small accomplishments of being able to speak with better pronunciation and moving his limbs slightly. The physiotherapist, Shawn, helped Tim sit up in his bed, stand for a second, and sit in a chair for about two hours. Shawn plans on having Tim walk for a bit tomorrow. Baby steps, we are reminded.

Tim's mental capacities are becoming more focused as his nurse asks him routine questions from who he is to where he is. He remembers his name and that he is in the hospital, yet he is unclear as to why. He figures his hospital stay has been between ten and twenty days. He notices the Valentine's Day balloons and realizes he has missed it. Tim is feeling happy and in good spirits. He wants to talk about his dreams and what he experienced during his coma. I find it amazing how Tim's intuitive muscle seems to be flexing, because it normally isn't. He begins to ask me different questions regarding "all of this Voodoo Shit" and what it all means. We chat a bit on this topic. I am happy to see him healing little by little, yet I am cautious not to be overly optimistic. Our boys come by with my mom to visit their dad also and they are very pleased to see him laughing and talking.

Why am I feeling numb? All my family is feeling relaxed, even Tim's disposition is better than mine. I place my mask on and smile throughout the day, although I am dumbfounded that I am not more content. It is probably because I have trained myself to regulate my emotional, spiritual, and energetic states to not deviate too much. What a ride it has been!

My clairvoyant tool shows me a vision of a new and improved Tim. He is living a healthy lifestyle, he is strong and active, and he is much happier while not being prone to anger. My gut intuits he will become more astute with his intuition and he will make more conscious, sustainable choices. I am starting to feel relieved, as my own intuition is reigniting and I become more at peace as each hour goes by.

The day ends on a positive note and everyone feels as though we can relax and be more at ease. Even I sleep better this evening.

Thursday, February 21, 2013—Put Your Dancing Shoes On

"It is worth dying to find out what life is."
T.S. Eliot

Upon my arrival bright and early, Tim is already awake and is crying. He is extremely grateful for being alive and well. He continues to speak of his experiences during his coma. They are not as heavenly as I have recently read from other patients who have had near-death experiences (NDEs). I insist that Tim try not to speak too much as I can tell his stats elevate as he recalls his dreams. I promise to bring him a journal and pen so he can record his NDE when he is able to hold a pen again or I can scribe for him until he builds up his strength. My intuitive muscle was indeed accurate, as I had figured he had travelled to a place we refer to as Hell, rather than the roads leading up to Heaven. As Tim was roaming his way through Hell during his coma, I was having my own experience, which I would not refer to as heavenly. It seemed a constant struggle of telling myself to remain positive and calm.

Being in a bed immobile for one day is equivalent to not exercising for one week. Tim was immobilized for ten days, not including the days prior to being in a coma. He will need a lot of time to rebuild his muscles, as he is still very weak. Holding a utensil is a challenge, as is sitting in a chair. Shawn, the physiotherapist, assures him that every day he will gain more mobility and we will see improvements even from hour to hour. It seems odd to see a grown man have to relearn how to do the simplest tasks from feeding himself to walking.

After breakfast, Tim sits in a chair for nearly two hours.

Shawn asks Tim if he'd like to take a walk. It's *a piece of pie*, I tell my husband, and he and Shawn laugh. I ask them what is so funny. Tim reminds me for the hundredth time that it is not *a piece of pie*, it's a piece of cake. Oh, what difference does it make! They are both sweet is my comeback.

I explain to Tim he'll do just fine as subconsciously he remembers how to walk, despite not feeling as though he knows how to in this moment. He agrees to give it a try while fighting off the tiredness he feels. Shawn is assisting Tim as he holds the walker and I follow with a wheelchair, just in case. Tim walks halfway down the hall and as he turns around he sees his parents standing at the other end of the hallway. Although being exhausted and wanting to sit in the comfort of the wheelchair, Tim forces himself to walk back to his room. I know he is doing this to impress his parents. With shaking arms holding tight onto the walker, Tim steadily drags his feet on the floor until he reaches his parents. This is a very proud moment for Tim, his parents, and me. Tim, as the child walking for the first time, his parents seeing their son walking again, and me witnessing the joy and pride. There's a round of applause for his accomplishment, then Tim crashes into bed for a well-deserved rest. Many changes continue throughout the day, as Tim is getting stronger. I am amazed as I watch subtle improvements in my husband's health.

I reflect on the conversations I had with the other families of ICU patients, when their relative was stepping down from the ward and I know what must have been going through their minds. I am astonished at the overwhelming feeling of intense joy I feel right at this moment. I am still tired as my sleep has been irregular and I notice that being filled with happiness or joy seems to take as much energy as being filled with hopelessness or fear. Perhaps I was numb on certain days during Tim's coma to not drain myself of my energy for this exact moment when he needs me the most, because when he slept in a coma, he rested; he did not need me. With him awake, alive, and more active each day, he needs me to assist him in performing daily chores, like brushing his hair. I hadn't realized that I could actually be more exhausted and tired as I am today.

Friday, February 22, 2013—Getting Closer to Home

"Life isn't about finding yourself. Life is about creating yourself."
George Bernard Shaw

Tim is moving around in his bed almost on his own. He is unable to get out of bed without assistance. He tells me this is his goal for today. I congratulate him on setting the first goal of his new lifetime. Reflecting back, we both realize that he had not set many goals for himself prior to this moment.

After his exercise with Shawn and sitting in the chair, Tim walks around the entire ICU ward. I nickname him "King of ICU." He is a superstar. The many nurses and RTs who have cared for him last week greet him and they are happy to see him walking about. Tim is beaming like a peacock showing off his feathers. He is very tired when he returns to his room and naps for a few hours. After his nap, Tim is quizzed, as he has been daily as to who he is, where he is, and what the date is. He cannot remember being in the hospital for as long as he has been. Tim looks down to his dated wristband, looks over to the Valentine's Day balloons (again), and looks to me asking if he has missed the Valentine's Day dance we had planned on attending. I answer yes, to which he realizes he has been in the hospital for most of the month of February. I am feeling quite blessed as Tim has not asked me yet why I chose not to "pull the plug." I hope we will never have to talk about it, although my intuitive thought is this dialogue will occur.

That afternoon, Tim wants to talk more about his near-death experience. I can see he is anxious to get his story heard. In spite of his overall confusion, the memory of his NDE is razor sharp. I listen attentively to each detail as Tim recalls his story. Through the anguish, the torture, and the hell he experienced, there are glimpses of light and love for which I am grateful. He recalls his spirit—his soul—floating away from his body at one point shortly after being intubated. He wonders what is responsible for making his spirit rise above and away from his body. I explain it is most likely a way for his soul to deal with the pain he was having on a physical level. On a spiritual level, I suspect it was his spirit taking a look "out there" and determining if it was his time to leave this physical plane we call Earth.

Tim asks me if I or anyone else tried to give him Reiki during his coma. I explain that Lynne, my Reiki Master, had attempted a few times without success. He wants to know why and what she felt. I tell him what Lynne shared with me. She had sensed a bubble around him and his refusal to receive the healing Reiki energy from her. Lynne also indicated he was making a decision. Tim's eyes well up with tears as he remembers the bubble around himself, which he had placed there to protect himself from the other people in his "dream." I let him know that a few days later, I was able to send him Reiki and my friend, Marina, was able to send him healing energy in the form of light and love adorned with symbols of hearts, roses, and infinity signs. Tim is unclear at the moment what an infinity sign looks like. He asks for the whiteboard and pen so he can draw the symbol he saw during his experience. He draws an infinity symbol. We smile at each other knowing his spirit and soul has felt all the healing, the love, and the light we sent him during his hellish time out. He continues to question me as he did two days ago on how to flex his intuitive muscle and wants to know more about all of this Voodoo Shit, which he for so long avoided.

I am told Tim will be returning to our hometown hospital this evening. I am a little apprehensive about leaving. We have seen at least two families come and go home with positive results during our stay in ICU. Now, it is our turn. Once we return to the Peace Arch Hospital, Tim will be placed in the ICU ward until the doctor assesses him and deems him fit to move into a step-down ward. Tim is very anxious to be moving as well. He is still a bit confused and still doesn't know exactly why he is in the hospital. Once the transfer team arrives late in the evening, I assure Tim that we will be right behind him and we will see him back at Peace Arch. He tells his nurse, Tejal that he likes it here and he doesn't want to leave. Tejal responds he is strong enough now and will be happier to be closer to home. Tim waves with tears in his eyes to the nurses and the rest of the Abbotsford ICU staff as they wave back and wish him a quick recovery.

Part Three
Tim and I Strengthen Our Inner Voodoo

Tim's Journey in Tim's Words

"You will learn (the good from the bad) when you are calm, at peace. Passive. A Jedi uses the Force for knowledge and defense, never for attack."
Yoda

Most accounts of NDEs are filled with peace, calm, love, and an everlasting sense of joy and awe. Having said this, not all people who are in a coma whether medically induced or otherwise, go through an NDE. I am a strong believer of life after death. I am an advocate for "out of the box" thinking, as I believe anything is possible and why not? Life can be so stressful and serious, why not add some flair and have fun with it. I am promising to live this way more often.

I had finished reading the book, *Proof of Heaven* by Eben Alexander months before Tim's illness. Dr. Alexander is a neurosurgeon who became infected with bacterial meningitis and was in a comatose state for seven days. As a man of science, he doubted the world of spirituality until he experienced it for himself. It pleased me as a highly spirited woman to read his book and to know such a reputable man could merge the two worlds together—science and spirituality. Without divulging too much of his book, Dr. Alexander describes, as most other NDE authors do, a world beyond Earth filled with indescribable light beings, magical sensations of flying on angel wings, and of a heavenly, greater source. Dr. Alexander also makes reference to a darker side he calls the "Earthworm's eye view." I suspect this was not the case for my husband. What I knew for sure was Tim did not experience this wonderfully, magical place that we refer to as Heaven during his NDE. He was Hellbound.

This part of the story is written through Tim's eyes and his viewpoint. One of the first words that Tim tried communicating was "Hell."

TIM'S JOURNEY THROUGH TIM'S EXPERIENCES

I open my eyes and I wonder where I am. I see my sister and my dad. Am I back in the real world, I question? Then, I hear Michèle's voice and I feel happy for the first time in what seems to be a long time. For now, I am safe. They tell me I am in a hospital and I am very sick. Everybody is very thrilled to see me awake. Their eyes fill with tears of joy.

They have no clue where I have been. My dad explains to me that I should not try to talk due to tubes being down my throat. I realize this fact quite quickly and try to pull the tubes out, to the displeasure of everyone. "You are awake ten minutes and you are already in trouble, Tim," my dad chuckles.

If you have not had tubes rammed down your throat, let me explain. You can't close your mouth fully and your mouth is very, very dry. You know when you wake up in the morning when you have a cold: your tongue feels like leather and your mouth is like the bottom of a birdcage. Try sleeping for a week... Thirsty, I am so thirsty. This thirst would not be quenched for another three days when they finally removed the tubes. The nurses were kind enough to rinse my mouth out with some foul mouthwash, old school Listerine, I think.

I so want to talk, so many unanswered questions. How long have I been here? Where is here? I must tell them about my journey, damn tubes… At least Dad has created a way to communicate with me through a whiteboard with the alphabet complete from A to Z. He has also added a spot with a "Yes" and a "No." I point to the letters H, E, L, L. I hear him say to Michèle, "I think he is trying to say—Hello."

I shake my head back and forth, indicating a resounding "No."

I try spelling "Hell" again. My dad puts the board aside in an effort to change the subject. I am back, I keep telling myself. I don't know exactly where I was for the past ten days, even though I don't realize it has been ten days. I am told this information much later on.

The last thing I know for certain is I was sitting in a wheelchair by myself and a nurse at the emergency ward was asking me for my name. I realize I don't know my name. I don't even know where I am or why I am here. How am I supposed to remember my name? Apparently, this is not normal behaviour and she takes this very seriously.

I get rushed into another room and everything goes black. I wake up later, a length of time that seems to be an hour, in a tube (a very small tube). It's a CT machine. I'm wearing only a hospital gown. I wonder how I got here. The voice from far away is telling me to stop moving around.

"Get me the hell out of here!"

Everything goes black, again. I awake again to a doctor's voice telling me I am very sick. I can see Michèle standing by my side. She asks me if she should call my family. I muster the strength to answer, "Yes."

The doctor continues to speak and informs me that I will be in-tubated and I have no clue what this means. I am told I will be sleeping. I ask weakly, "For how long?"

He replies, "A few days." I think to myself, I could use the sleep. I am so tired, I have been so sick for about a week with what we think is the flu. I say 'bye to my family with tears in my eyes. My journey begins…

I am in a small, smoky store and I've just purchased a ritual gown. People surround me and they are painting my body with murals. I don't recognize or know any of these people. A woman tells me that I need to speak to a priestess. I don't quite understand why I need to do this. I realize my dad is upset with me, because I spent so much money on this ceremonial gown and he thinks I joined a cult. His disappointment hurts me, but for some weird reason, I need to do this. I leave the store through the back door down a dark hallway. When I open the door, the sky is a menacing red and there is a massive pyramid before me. There is a winding path with a steep drop on either side. I guess this is the way to the priestess. I follow the path. I am not aware of time anymore, minutes, hours, weeks, eternity; it is all the same now. I enter the pyramid through endless corridors in search of the priestess, not knowing what she looks like or what to expect. This is stupid. The whole time I wonder how I can ever make up with my dad. I continue walking. I end up back outside the pyramid, disappointed, and wondering if I have failed my task. I never did see or speak to the priestess. The funny thing is none of this seemed weird.

I don't know how I am transported from place to place. Sometimes, I open a door. Other times, I just open my eyes. It is kind of like dreaming that you are dreaming, if you can imagine that.

The next place I am in is a hospital bed with my dad at my side. There is a digital sign in front of me, the kind you see at a corner store advertising candy. It reads, "El loco gringo, we are coming to get you." I ask my dad what this means and if this message is for me. He replies, "Don't worry, everything is fine." I have memories of a drug deal gone badly, like a scene right out of the movies.

Dad and I are speeding down a dirt road in an old pickup truck. I inform my dad that when we get home, I will Google this and try to figure this shit out. What the hell do you type in the search field for this info? I feel extremely confused. "Why am I in a hospital in Mexico?" I wonder to myself.

I get bounced to another place, another scene, where I am in another hospital bed in a different room. My wife Michèle is curled up at my feet, sleeping. I feel the presence of a man behind me whispering in my ear, "Don't worry, everything will be okay, you're next."

This is no hospital; we seem to be in a kitchen. The lights are flickering and everything is wet, like it was just sprayed with a fire hose. Two dark figures enter the room and take Michèle away. I have a bad feeling about this. I can hear her pleading, "No, please no!" She is begging for her life.

I try to get up but nothing works. The voice again says, "Don't worry, you are next." Don't worry! Who is this person? They are killing my wife and you say, "Don't worry."

Her screams stop. I feel this unbearable feeling of loss. All I can do is weep in my bed with this stranger behind me. I ask, "Why are you doing this?" No one answers. A figure rolls out a serving cart with an elegant meal prepared on it. Candles are lit; he is ready to serve this meal to the guests of this creepy restaurant.

Scene change... I am in a room, in a different hospital and I have the worst thirst I have ever had. A can of Coca-Cola appears in front of me. The voice behind me says, "Have a drink." I tell him I have no money and I can't pay for the drink. "Don't worry, you can pay later," I am told.

Deep down I realize he wants more than I can give him. He appears to want my soul. I am curious to know whose voice I keep hearing whispering behind me. It is not a voice I recognize. "Who is this man?" I keep asking myself. I drift away.

I wake up looking at a big screen TV in my room. He asks if I like the TV and again I inform him that I cannot pay for this. Why am I being tempted with objects that I can't pay for? I can't seem to understand what is going on. Drifting away once more, I come back and my room is empty. I get up out the bed and wander outside into the darkness. I sense fear building up within me. In my confusion, I think, "Where will I go next?"

I now realize I have memories of the past places I have visited. You know, after you wake up from a bad dream, you tell yourself, "It was just a bad dream; go back to sleep." I don't get to wake up. Am I just dreaming?

I appear to be in an elevator shaft going down, but I cannot be sure. There are people looking through the glass doors at me. The doors open and the crowd is angry because I am here. I tell them I am lost and I don't know where I am or why I am here. They do not offer to help me. In the meantime, I shake my head back and forth very violently in an attempt to get out of here.

I return to my hospital bed, again. I open my eyes and I read another sign in my room. The sign reads, "The Hells Angels donated this wing of the hospital."

I figured this was weird, but then again, everything else has been too. Why am I in a Hells Angels' hospital? Why will no one explain to me what is happening? I don't understand and I am very confused. Fear is starting to set in. Where is my family? Why am I alone? "Has anyone seen my dad or my wife," I yell out.

No one hears me.

I can hear the rev of a motorcycle arriving. I overhear a conversation. Someone wants to use the room that I am in. The doctor says a patient is using the room; that patient is me. Suddenly, I notice my wife standing beside me and I question her, "What is the commotion all about?"

She replies, "Everything will be fine."

Why does everyone keep telling me that, when clearly everything is not fine?

The bikers are arguing loudly outside my room. They proclaim that I should not be there; they have paid for the hospital and I need to leave. I ask my wife where our boys are. Her reply is that they are at school. How can they be at school when I can hear the boys screaming? Where are they, I ask myself? I feel so helpless lying in the hospital bed. I hear our boys scream again and I know the bikers are beating them up. I tell this to Michèle and she repeats that everything will be okay. Does anyone understand that everything is not fine! Why can't she hear the boys screaming? Why does she persist in telling me everything is fine?

I need to get out of here; this can't be happening!

I tell myself to shake my head again to get myself out of this situation. I am moved to another hospital room where a doctor is violently ramming hoses down my throat. I am chained tightly to the bed and I see blood drip from my wrists. He is enjoying what he is doing. I am not and I am scared. He places a folded piece of paper on the nightstand and leaves me in agony. Later on, a nurse arrives and asks me how I am doing. I can't reply as tubes are down my throat. She wants to know how much I paid for this procedure. How the hell am I to know that? I am so confused and scared… She looks around the room and spots the piece of paper. Walking toward the nightstand, she takes the paper, unfolds it, and shouts out, "This is ridiculous! The doctor has charged you $10,000 for this."

She storms out of the room in search of the doctor. Once she finds him, I can hear them argue; the doctor returns and does a motion across his neck with his thumb while looking at me. Why would he kill me? Or does he mean that I am going to die? Again, I am so confused and scared. The nurse decides to call the police and, before they arrive, the doctor kills the nurse. He enters my room with the knife he just killed the nurse with. He states I will regret what I have done. What have I done, I wonder? The police arrive. In a hail of bullets, the doctor dies. Another doctor arrives in my room; he says he'll take me somewhere safe, his house where I can rest. Rest? Am I not sleeping?

When we arrive at his house, the new doctor places me in a dark, closed-in closet. I am hanging by rusty chains on the wall of the closet. The floor is missing from the closet and nuclear, green waste bubbles up from below. I can see a woman below in the gooey mess. I think it is his mother. She is pushing a broom through this waste; she appears to be trying to clean it up. I call out to her and she ignores me. I manage to get unhooked and I run down the dark street wondering where to go. I enter another hospital and find a room with a bed to lie in and rest. I am so tired and frightened.

After I have had what appears to be a very long sleep, a huge man enters my room. He is muscular, bald, and black. He looks like a cartoon action figure. His name is Sweet. He professes to be my protector. He has two enormous pistols in his hands. He says, "Don't tell anyone I am here as they are all trying to kill you."

Who do I trust, the doctors or him? I can hear footsteps coming up the hall. Sweet tells me he will hide in the closet of my room. The doctor asks me if anyone entered my room. I ignore him and he leaves. He returns with an army of security guards. He informs me they will take care of everything. They weld the closet door shut and leave. Sweet is stuck inside as he bangs on the door and cries out. I can't help him. Eventually, the screaming and the banging stop. What happened to Sweet? I feel so alone. Again, fear is rising within my chest.

I shake my head with all my might; as this is the only way I know to get out. The only trouble with this is I never know where I will land. I am back at the creepy restaurant. Michèle is on my lap and she needs to leave. I beg her not to go, as they will eat her. She laughs and playfully touches my cheek. Once she is gone, I can hear her screaming in agony. What is happening to her? Why couldn't she just stay here as I asked? She returns to my room covered in burning, hot chocolate with her skin peeling off her bones. Don't they know that Michèle is allergic to chocolate? Why have they covered her like this? As she walks toward me, the chocolate is hardening and she falls to the floor, dead, again. The male voice reassuring me from behind says, "Everything is going to be okay."

"How can you say that? Look at my wife. She is dead! Why am I being so tormented?" I do not understand and I am scared.

I shake my head again; I need to get out of here. I don't want to see Michèle dead. I wake up in a dark underground garage beside a desk where a faceless nurse is busily typing on the computer. I ask her why I am here; she states, "They are coming to get you."

"Who?" I ask.

She doesn't answer. After a while the nurse finally speaks. "They are here now. Prepare yourself."

I ask, "How do I prepare myself when I don't even know what I am preparing myself for?"

She replies in a serious, yet gentle tone, "Think of love and light."

Before me appears a very dirty, old, and cracked mirror which I look at. I do not see my reflection. Instead, I see a symbol. The symbol appears to be an awareness ribbon for cancer or something like that. The nurse advises me to not stop staring into the symbol and to continue to think of love and light. She reassures me that I will be okay.

A car arrives. Three masked people get out. One at a time, they line up behind me. The nurse reminds me to think of love and light. "Continue to look at the symbol," she firmly says.

I strain my mind to think of love and light, and to concentrate on the symbol in the mirror as a bubble forms around me. The first masked person has a gun and tries to shoot three bullets into my brain. I feel pressure as each bullet bounces off my head. He leaves in frustration. His masked partner tries to kill me as well with a huge sword. Sparks fly as the sword makes contact with me. He leaves not completing his assignment of killing me. The third masked assailant tries to smash my head with a big hammer without success. He also leaves as I continue to concentrate on the symbol and think of light and love. They enter their car and drive off. The nurse tells me everything will be fine now.

Now all this happened over twelve days, but time was not present during this, this dream...

I open my eyes and I see my sister and my dad and I hear Michèle's voice. My dad shows me the chart he has made adorned with the alphabet. He informs me I am in hospital, very sick with tubes down my throat, so I shouldn't talk. He shows me the chart with the alphabet and I point to the letters spelling "Hell." Now you know why this was my first word.

After that journey, I became painfully aware of just how lucky I am.

Unplugged and Plugged In

"Not everyone is meant to make a difference. But for me, the choice to lead an ordinary life is no longer an option."
Peter Parker

Tim spent another week or so in the hospital as he built up his strength each day. He remained on oxygen and was slowly unplugged from IV lines and other gadgets as the week went by. He was not allowed to leave the hospital until he no longer required oxygen and most of the infection had gone from his lungs. Tim continued to walk throughout the halls of the much smaller ward and he was told he couldn't leave the floor. I continued to assist him with daily routines as he was rather weak and I sensed it would be at least another month until he can be left alone at home. In the meantime, my mother returned to Ontario before Tim was released from the hospital. With Tim in the regular ward, we could no longer hold twenty-four-hour vigils. He felt strange sleeping without his dad watching over him. We joked and advised Tim that his roommate was holding the vigil. He still questioned us and wanted to know the source of his illness. We persisted to inform him that he suffered a severe and deadly pneumonia. I made a mental note to tell my husband which disease caused his demise. We celebrated the day he became "unplugged," just as an artist re-releases his cover album.

His inner Voodoo power, gut instincts, intuition increased dramatically after he awoke. He became fully "plugged into" his intuitive muscle. He could hear the wind blowing outside despite the windows being shut tight. His taste buds went into high gear, he noticed synchronicities, and his awareness became more fine-tuned. He repeatedly expressed gratitude for most items we take for granted each day, such as drinking water, holding a pen, tasting food, speaking, being able to walk, and more importantly breathing. His gratitude made me rethink what I am truly grateful for also.

One quiet afternoon as Tim and I sat reading, he stared out the window and noticed the windowsill was covered with ladybugs. I had seen these during the first few days at Peace Arch Hospital in the ICU ward. I sensed Tim's intuition was buzzing. I waited silently, wondering what he'd do or say next. Still peering at the window, Tim stated it was strange and peculiar to have ladybugs littering the windowsill at the end of February. I agreed, not saying more than necessary, and I waited. Finally, Tim looked in my eyes intensely and with a serious voice asked me what "ladybug" means "intuitively." Oh, if he only knew, I thought to myself. I did not tell Tim that ladybug spirit has already appeared. Their initial visit (if you will) was strictly intended for me. This visit, my gut was telling me, was for my husband. As the good teacher, I asked Tim what he thought the message might be. He pondered, reflected, and stated he believed they were trying to tell him to become more in tune with his intuition and be more content.

Just as Yoda was proud of his student, Luke in *Star Wars*, I was pleased with my husband. I tell him ladybug spirit means, "Something you thought was lost will be making its way back into your life. You're being called upon to increase your spiritual or devotional practices. You want to release fears and anxieties, and return to feeling trusting and happy."

Tim smiled and full-heartedly agreed with these messages. The something he lost was himself before our separation and his life (while he was in a coma). He definitely wanted to get back to a happy place in his life and feel no more fear. Tim explained he was experiencing everything he did for the first time—all over again. He claimed to have taken so much for granted in the past and he professed to do the opposite, to be more appreciative, aware, and attentive. He restated how the first piece of ice tasted magical when he was finally able to have it after nearly twelve days of not drinking. I could tell he was not enjoying his hospital food and I advised him it was fine to leave it. I offered him my fruit smoothie drink instead. He graciously accepted and confessed it felt ungrateful to not eat his hospital breakfast. To put my husband at ease, I ate his breakfast and recommended for the next day's breakfast we order tea and toast. He smiled as he sipped, enjoying the smoothie while I ate his cold eggs.

Lastly, his supersonic internal vision became razor sharp as he recalled every minute detail of his hellish near-death experience. He questioned me on several subjects concerning meditation, mediumship, Reiki, dreams, and their meanings. For the first time, I truly knew my husband respected the work I do with my clients in mentoring them, in flexing their intuitive muscles, and he understood the validity and importance of following your own gut instincts, your inner Voodoo, your spidey-senses, your intuition.

I Thought I Was Off This Ride!

"My grandma has this saying: Trust those who seek the truth but doubt those who say that they have found it."
Hannah McKay, Dexter, Season 7, Episode 7

Everyone's life goes back to normal after a crisis. My parents-in-law went back to their home with their dog and continued enjoying the quiet, island lifestyle. My sisters-in-law went back to work and no longer needed to call every day to inquire on Tim's health and well-being. Shortly after returning home from the hospital, the house was quiet and perhaps uneasy. Shamus, our dog, greeted Tim with trepidation until his master finally spoke. Our dog instinctively knew his master was better. He followed Tim around the whole house for the first week back home, making sure he was fine. The dog didn't jump on Tim, as he normally would, yet chose to walk alongside him as his protector. The telephone stopped ringing off the hook, as all our relatives and friends were assured of Tim's improving condition. Some still offered to help yet they were not sure what the help would look like. Nor was I. I felt as though I needed the help yet I didn't know what it looked like. Even, my parents did not call for their weekly check-up on Tim anymore.

It was much like when you are new parents and everyone calls to see how the baby is doing. They never bother to ask how the parents are doing. Well, this mirrored my life somewhat. Tim was the new baby and I was the parent. I consistently answered questions about how Tim was doing. I did not mind, as I was pleased to have my husband back and recovering, although, I was falling apart inside and no one seemed to notice. I continued to wear my mask of the wife who is eternally grateful and pleased to have her husband back.

Have you ever noticed that people say the most inappropriate things when you are suffering? For instance, I heard the expressions, "Life is so short…" and "You should never take anything for granted" and "Only time heals…" on more occasions than I cared to hear them after Tim and I got home from the hospital. In general, people are trying to be kind, sympathetic, and understanding. Yet, how can they be if they haven't gone through the same event as you? It was difficult for me to keep my faith from wavering as internally I was crashing and became a basket case. All I needed was a hug and a shoulder to cry on for a long time. Why did I feel so abandoned?

What no one knew, including Tim, is that I was grieving. I didn't even know I was grieving until I went out socially for the first time in three months. I sat beside a lovely woman and we begin to chat. She told me she was branching out to start her own business as a grief counsellor. I wished her the best and, out of the blue—I got this one right—I shared a bit of what had happened during the month of February. She suggested taking me as a pilot client and I welcomed the help.

At our initial session, she assessed my stress level. Apparently, the red zone is 250+; my stress scale measured at 650! Yikes, this is dangerously high! She implemented various exercises I must do to reduce my stress as soon as possible. Some of them I had already been doing, as they are similar to the exercises I provide my clients with in highly charged and stressful scenarios.

My clairaudient tool was hearing I need time to heal now. I was really beginning to despise time. Once again, I was face-to-face with time or was it a boxing match! Couldn't time fly by and my life be back to normal? Normal, what is normal? Was it the normalcy, mundaneness of routines I sought? I was not quite certain.

I almost did not feel any different from when I sat watching my husband in a coma. Just as I thought life was crashing in

February, it was still crashing at full force three months later. I was at an impasse, a roadblock, or was it a crossroad? Old feelings from past relationships crept up and haunted me. I couldn't make a decision to save my life, albeit three months before, the decision I made had saved my husband's life. Again, the irony set in. I was losing control of who I was. Was I my husband's caregiver? Was I Wonder Woman who has all the balls juggling in the air? I no longer knew who I was and I recognized I was suffering from caregiver's crash and burnout.

I wouldn't say I was depressed, although I will most definitely tell you I was upset, angry, irritated, annoyed, outraged, and downright pissed off. "How could this be?" I asked myself, second by second, minute by minute. The damn concept of time was killing me. When time was passing by excruciatingly slowly in the hospital, I sat watching the lines on the monitors slither like a snake, wishing for time to speed up so that traumatic, critical event could be over. Again, time was in slow motion and I felt just as alone suffering in silence, hearing the tick-tock of the clock.

When sentiments are at an all-time low, it is difficult to recognize the good. For instance, we had just moved in the early summer to a house with a big backyard, an ocean view from our deck, and a beautiful park across the street. This was as close to my dream home as I had visualized in a meditation and I couldn't even appreciate the goodness, the manifestation of the dream. The reason was simply because I was in a low state, feeding my emotions with anger, grief, and denial.

At a session with my grief counsellor two months later, I confessed to her I was utterly fuming, because Tim did not die. I was shocked as I heard the words come out of my mouth without hesitation. How dare he put me through that whole critical situation and not die! I had gone through every damn emotion of a widow, yet Tim sat there enjoying life. This seemed so ridiculous. I urged myself to be happy and to get rid of the anger and disappointment. I knew it wasn't healthy to be stewing in those feelings. I felt deceived by God, because Tim had not died. I'd expected him to die following the same symbol of death that appeared to me for so long, from you, God! What if God replied, "It is not My fault, Michèle. You didn't get it."

This angered me to the core. I was willing to accept my life without my husband. I am outraged at You—God, at Tim, at the powers that be! All of you have made me furious. My intuitive, intelligent, and composed self would ask me, "Why allow others to upset you?"

I wanted to take control of my own emotions, feel them, allow life through them, quickly, and let them go! Enough of the *Peanutting comments*, I don't want to hear them any longer.

My grief counsellor advised me to find the treasure, the hidden message, the gift and the lesson in the critical event. I did not want to or was it that I was not ready to? Either way, I was not thrilled with this session and I told her. She apparently thought this was good. It wasn't feelings of fear or uneasiness; it was simply, I just don't want to! I intuitively heard with my clairaudient tool that I was behaving like a two-year-old. "So?" I replied back.

The fight, the name-calling, the pointing of the finger, the blame could persist. I decided to own it, to stand in my power, and to stop. This did not mean I would get up out of the shit pile I was stuck in. On the contrary, I sat silently in the shit with my arms crossed over my chest and my heart. This was my way to demonstrate to my intuition I didn't want to see, hear, feel, or know it was present within me.

We all have these crappy moments. We can see the pile of crap ahead. Do we decide to walk around it, jump over it, go through it, or sit in it? That day, I chose to sit in it. As a healer, I know I should have gone around it or at least acknowledged I shall only sit in it for a short while, recognize I hate the stink, get up quickly, and move on. Instead, I decided to sit in the pile of crap for longer. Basically, I was not ready to learn the lesson, see the light at the end of tunnel, and find the hidden message or gift from the events of February. My counsellor sympathetically said it was fine and when the time to get up arrived, I would get up fast, shake it off, and move on quickly. I certainly hoped she was correct, because it stunk in there!

I have not worked since the beginning of February 2013 when I brought Tim to the hospital. Did I advise my clients that I would be out of commission for a while? I was scheduled to teach a Reiki class. Did I even postpone it? Through the fogginess and my trance-like state from this past month, I don't remember what I did outside of staying at the hospital. I was functioning on autopilot for so long that I am in a complete haze. My whole life was put on hold until my husband's health was regained. I eventually have to go back to work, because money doesn't *grow in bushes*.

The initial day I returned to work, I was hugged by a client who asked me how my husband was doing and I broke down into full sobs. I apologized for my lack of professionalism and getting his shirt wet with my tears. He told me to forget about the mascara-stained shirt and we talked about my journey for a while. My client is my friend. He sat attentively listening to my story relating resonating messages to his life's journey as it filled him with great insight and clarity. He shared with me how humbling it was to hear that I too stumbled with my intuition during trying times. I responded to him that this is the time when we most need our intuition in guiding us through uncharted territory.

After my client's session was finished, I noticed my body was relaxed and was healing. I smiled a little to myself, as I was pleased to feel I was finally healing. Through my healing sessions of working with my grief counsellor, receiving Reiki, massage therapy, meditation, yoga, and working with my clients as their personal intuitive trainer, I have healed myself. The healer is healed.

I have no jurisdiction in determining when Tim will die. I expected him to die and I never talked about it with Tim. How could I? "By the way, honey, I have this vision that you die before you are forty-five years old."

I avoided the topic of my intuitive muscle flexing this thought. Was it to prepare myself for … for what? For this day of deception! For me to doubt my inner Voodoo power, my spidey-senses, my gut instincts, my intuition, which has guided me for so long. It has been my trusted and true friend my whole life, never once leading me in the wrong direction. Was I deceived by my beliefs? This thought was so intensely painful it struck the very essence of who I am. My intuition had become so bloody fuzzy that I couldn't see through the fog. I was wearing mud-covered glasses. What was my role in the world? Do I continue with the work I was doing with my clients, mentoring them in fine-tuning their intuition, when clearly I was doubtful and lacking confidence in my own abilities? I felt like a hypocrite. How could I maintain healthy mentoring relationships with my clients as their personal intuitive trainer when my intuition had shattered? Why was this so ironic? I was the gifted intuitive whose very own intuition was fractured, out of shape, and severely damaged. The whole essence of who I thought I was, of who I am was destroyed, and it was agonizing to look in the mirror.

Speaking of the mirror … have you ever noticed that when you are in a particular state, good or bad, others around you seem to be reflecting similar situations, emotions, and sentiments? They are reflecting the traits, characteristics, emotions, and so forth that are the strongest in us at that moment. This is referred to as "Mirror Relationships."

This is comparable to when you are thinking or have just purchased a new car. For the sake of this exercise, the vehicle is the newest Mini Cooper (which, by the way, is my favourite car). Suddenly, you are driving to work, to home, running errands, or cruising about with the top down enjoying the wind blowing in your hair on a warm sunny evening. Everywhere you drive your Mini Cooper you encounter other Mini Coopers. They are in your awareness, in your consciousness. This is no different from mirror relationships.

I had doubted my intuition, despite my acute skills, and I was physically exhausted. Every person I dealt with over the course of a couple of months following my husband's near-death experience was either always tired and/or doubting their intuition. It hit me like a ton of bricks sitting on the couch one afternoon with a client when he professed his distrust in his inner Voodoo, his intuition. I thought this confusing, as this particular client always demonstrated refined intuitive skills that matched mine. I stopped him mid-sentence and questioned why he would think this. His reply was he had trusted his gut for as long as he could remember and, all of a sudden, it seemed to shut down. I dug further, asking more questions to find the root of his thinking. We continued to converse this way, until he stopped me in my tracks. Pointing his finger and shouting, "Aha! This conversation is for you, Michèle. I am your mirror!"

As I mentioned before, I was hit in the face with the mirror or did it smash me over the head? Either way, it served as a wake-up call for me not only to snap out of this slump, but also it helped me to take an inventory of my toolbox, reacquaint myself with my tools, and start using them one by one, once more. Furthermore, I regained confidence in my abilities as I realized they had never faded away. I had only chosen to place my intuition, my gut instincts, on the back burner instead of allowing my intuition to guide me with grace and ease as it had done so many times before. My client was undeniably correct, one-hundred percent confirming!

Reflecting back over the previous month, I realized each of my clients had expressed corresponding speculation of their spidey-senses. This particular reflection was for me to reawaken my positive emotions and to stop beating myself up for an event that had been entirely out of my control. Essentially, the negative qualities circulating in my mind were being reflected in other people I dealt with on a regular basis so I could become aware of them within myself. We experience positive and negative emotions and feelings our whole life. At times, directed at others or us. Mirror relationships are a way for your intuition to hand over a powerful tool in dealing with emotional freedom and release.

What was the purpose of the symbolism behind the death? The symbol of death can mean so much. Was it Tim's transformation, the renewal of our relationship, the renewal of our marriage, or my further evolution? It can mean, perhaps, the death of a career to bring about self-employment; the end of one relationship to find your soul mate. In addition, it can mean an emotional death of letting go of old habits and an inner journey. If you are living in a state of unawareness, as though you are a zombie, are you already dead inside? It is only when we are faced with death that we truly see what is before us.

Tim has definitely gone through a major change. He described himself as being parallel to the main character of the brilliant HBO TV series *Dexter*. Dexter himself is a blood splatter expert with the Miami police and a serial killer who is a vigilante. He struggles to find balance by fitting into the real and normal world while portraying this image of a regular, shy guy. Dexter always says that he is carrying a dark passenger along with him. Tim stated that his dark passenger (who has been with him for a long time prior to his coma) has finally left him; therefore, his death was a metamorphosis of his inner demons. He promised to himself, not to me, not to our children, but rather to himself to be the best man he can be. He wanted to live a long, fruitful, and happy life filled with good health and a stronger intuitive muscle. Tim has learned to ask for help when he needs it and has realized that our bodies are not only physical, they are emotional and energetic, too. He fills his self-talk with positive thoughts and tries to eliminate the unnecessary mind chatter. He is quick to recognize when the light at the end of the tunnel is fading and he immediately takes action to relight the fire. He has even found his passion, which he could not identify beforehand. He acknowledges his self-worth by setting and attaining his goals. Tim knows he is not perfect as no one is; however, he does strive to be excellent each and every day.

One Year Later

"When your desires are strong enough, you will appear to possess superhuman powers to achieve."
Napoleon Hill

Tim's Words

I had such a weird day today. I told Michèle I had to sit down at work, because I got emotional and a little dizzy, my stomach full of butterflies.

"Don't you know what today is?" Michèle asks.

"No, I don't."

"Today is the anniversary of the day you came out of the coma."

Before, I told you I was lucky, and I am. I didn't think that way previously. I like myself now; easy to say, tough to do. It's more than family or relationships; it's about yourself and yourself only; and without self-worth you are doomed.

People ask, "Did you learn anything from your experience?"

I say, "Life is not perfect, but it's not supposed to be."

Want to make God laugh? Tell Him what you have planned for your life.

Michèle's Words

As for our marriage, it is much better than it was over one year ago. We communicate openly with one another, take time to appreciate moments being alone and being good parents. Mostly, we have changed the language we use. Our words are gentle, more filled with love, and we are not quick to anger. We only say what we mean and refrain from purposely hurting each other. Tim and I laugh more often and we recognize the worth in truly living life to its fullest. We still have the not-so-great moments in our relationship; yet the major difference is there are fewer of them and they resolve quickly. We do not let things stir and bubble in the pot or burn. We promised to address a situation when it does not feel right. Overall, we support and respect our efforts and we have fun.

My transformation has been overwhelming, as I stated earlier, from questioning who I am, my purpose in the world, and my intuitive muscle. I have learned from this ordeal to recognize whose business I am in, thanks to my grief counsellor. I ask myself, "Is it my business or is it their business?"

If it is their business, I will not allow feelings to overcome my overall state of being and cause me great discomfort. Not everyone will be on the same path as I am and that is fine. "The Serenity Prayer" by American theologian, Reinhold Niebuhr, brings me relief as I read, "Grant me the serenity to accept the things I cannot change, the courage to change the things I can, and the wisdom to know the difference."

If it is my business, I will deal with my emotions accordingly, take actions to shift my thinking, and employ the tips and tools I have in my toolbox to resolve the situation. I know that I am the same person as before the trauma, yet I am more evolved. Ultimately, I ask myself again, "Is Tim death's my business?"

My clairaudient tool firmly says no. I trust it fully this time around. Throughout these past few months, I have gained new skill sets I can use and I will continue to fill my toolbox.

One year later, I have been feeling tired for two weeks prior to February. I knew exactly why my body has given signs of this approaching day. I had experienced migraines, lack of sleep, weepiness, and an overall unstable emotional state. It is as though my body is reminding me that I went through this critical ordeal last year. Only time heals wounds. This is indeed a wound, a death of some sort that needed to heal.

Our family physician asked how I was doing during a follow-up appointment with Tim; I replied that I was definitely feeling as though Tim had actually died. My emotional, spiritual, and physical bodies did not know the difference. The grieving process I underwent was a reflection of someone who was widowed. The feelings, sentiments, emotions that surged and flowed through me were no different. I allowed them to bubble over and I made sure that I felt every one to the fullest. I needed to have time pass by quickly. After feeling my intuition announce a death for so long, I then wanted these emotions to be over. Yet, I was wrong. They did not disappear magically off into the sunset. Rather, they lingered and became stronger and new emotions emerged. My inner Voodoo power was advising me to allow myself to relive the past just a little so I could interpret any new sensations, emotions, and intuitiveness I needed to help me move forward. I did indeed follow and trust my intuition fully and found in the end it all worked out beautifully.

Realizing my intuition is as natural as breathing, I take a deep breath in through my nose and exhale with a sigh through my mouth. I can feel the air flow steadily through my lungs with grace and ease, as it should. I do not feel fear anymore concerning Tim's looming death. We are all scheduled to die and I have accepted this fact. A light bulb goes on. My claircognizant tool—my gut—is telling me this is what I feared: my life without being able to trust my spidey-senses, my gut instincts, my inner Voodoo power, my intuition. Over the next few days that pass by, my intuitive muscle continues to flex. My X-ray vision, my clairvoyant tool, showed me in a recent meditation that I am strong and can survive any critical event set before me as I climb to the mountaintop. My bionic, clairaudient hearing is picking up conversations of widows who find love again. So I do not fear this will happen to me anymore, as love may be possible. I am prepared to live my life even if Tim does die before me. Besides, Tim's spirit will always look over our boys and me. In my heart, I feel comfort knowing this to be true. As I sit on my deck enjoying the sunrise one morning, I think of the next phase of our life. My claircognizant tool is keenly active as a smile comes across my lips and I feel like dancing, no matter what is in store. I am reassured as my intuition—my trusted friend—has never abandoned me.

Tim also demonstrated flashback memories precisely one year after being in the hospital. He was at work climbing a ladder and suddenly felt extremely dizzy. He gently climbed down the ladder and sat in a nearby chair. He closed his eyes and a flood of memories came flowing through his mind. He saw himself sitting on the front steps outside our house getting sick; he remembered his good friend Jeff saying, "You don't look good, brother;" and then, as though a movie was playing in his head, the whole stay of his hospitalization flashed before his mind's eye. We spoke about it that night and he reread my journal from those twenty plus days in the hospital. He reread his journal of his dreams during his time-out. Even the children were tired on this day, one year later. Odd how our intuition, our subconscious state of mind, recalls what we don't necessarily know is right in front of us. I have spoken individually with the boys to inquire how they are feeling this year, knowing they almost lost their dad last year. Boys will be boys and less is more with them.

"Yah, we remember."

"Yah, we're doing fine." These were their replies. Yet, I know subconsciously they have gained valuable intuitive tools they will never forget.

Epilogue

"Happiness is when what you think, what you say, and what you do are in harmony."
Mahatma Gandhi

Throughout this book, I have given you many tips and tools that can assist you in flexing your intuitive muscle. My hope is that you have realized you are very powerful, you are Superman, you are Wolverine, you are Iron Man... You have an intuitive muscle that is worth flexing and using each day of your life. You have seen through my personal stories, my clients' experiences, through the lives of my three boys, and my husband's journey to Hell and back that your intuition never fails you, never leaves your side. Your intuition may be subtle and be speaking as softly as a whisper during turbulent phases. You can see, hear, feel, and know your intuition is there every step of the way through the struggles, the hardships, and the traumatic events even if you are not totally aware of its presence. Rest assured it is there and, with the assistance of a personal intuitive trainer like me, you too can clearly see, hear, feel, and know the signs of your intuitive muscle flexing.

Your superpower, your inner Voodoo Shit, your intuition comes in many different tools that you can pull out of your toolbox in any given moment. Your clairvoyant tool is what you see in your mind's eye, through dreams and visions, and what you are aware of in the physical world. Your clairaudient tool is your ability to hear messages from your supersonic ears. Your intuition is communicating through noises, sounds, words, and music to enlighten you through melodies. Your clairsentient tool is a way your body talks to you, intuitively. How are you feeling in this moment? Notice tension in your shoulders when you are being warned or a smile on your face when you are being guided to take on an adventure full-heartedly. Your clair-cognizant tool answers your burning question through your magical, instantaneous thoughts appearing out of the blue.

Through the implementation of different exercises, you will notice your intuitive muscle becomes stronger and more refined each day, exercises such as meditation and relaxation techniques to quiet your mind, boost your immunity, ease stress, increase creativity and productivity. Journaling is a form of keeping track of your dreams and recording your gifts of gratitude in an effort to increase your appreciation of life; daily journaling brings awareness to your experiences. Even medi-umship can be useful in communicating with loved ones who have passed over, as they too care deeply for your well-being and can provide valuable information in helping you take the next steps in your life. Treat yourself to a Reiki session with me or hire a personal intuitive trainer to help you gain clarity and insight. Just as with any other sport or ability, you must use your intuition to keep it healthy and fit.

There is so much more I wanted to cover in this book; I have just scratched the surface of the subject of intuition. However, what I have provided is a good foundation for you to start flex-ing your intuitive muscle. After reading this book and trying the exercises, you should be more comfortable with your abili-ties to gather intuitive, reliable information and put it to good use. You will find as you use each technique and tool more frequently, you will begin to personalize them for your own benefit and possibly use them for family members and friends. As I instructed at the beginning of the book, get out of your head, let go of judgments and perfection.

My husband was his own worst enemy by doubting his intui-tive voice constantly throughout his life. Learn from his errors; learn from other men's stories that I have shared—stories about my clients who are just like you. Use this book as a preventative tool to avoid making major mistakes in your personal and business life. Use this book as a reminder to take time to slow down and smell the roses, appreciate the beauty the world has to offer, become aware, educated, and conscious of your surroundings. Do not fear change, as change is the only constant in life. Deepak Chopra spoke these very true and resonating words. Life is all about change. The world is constantly changing around us; so do not be left behind. Change and evolve with the world. Stretch yourself a bit outside your comfort zone to try each exercise stated in this book and you will be pleasantly surprised as to how powerful and empowered you really are, because you are Superman!

Postscript

"If you realize that all things change, there is nothing you will try to hold on to. If you are not afraid of dying, there is nothing you cannot achieve."
Lao Tzu

Back to Abbotsford Hospital

There was one final step in my healing journey I needed to take. It was to return to Abbotsford General Hospital with Tim in his healthy state. We decided to go visit the hospital in March 2014. The car ride to Abbotsford was quiet as neither one of us spoke and the radio blared out "Die Young." I laughed at the irony of the song's lyrics as I sang along without a tear rolling down my cheek this time.

As we pull into the parking lot of the hospital, Tim asks me how I am doing. I reply, "Fine."

The moment we enter the massive front lobby, I look away embarrassed by the automatic flow of tears flooding my eyes. Tim continues to be impressed by the sheer size and newness of the hospital that he does not notice my tears. I stop walking as we approach the elevator that will bring us to the ICU ward. Sensing my uneasiness, Tim backs up, places his arm around my shoulders and suggests we go check out the cafeteria first. Tucking in my shirt like a big girl, I wipe the tears from my cheeks and wonder why I haven't brought tissues with me. I knew it would be emotional to walk through the ICU ward, yet I hadn't expected to break down in sobs in the lobby of the hospital.

I give Tim the grand tour—the green space, the pond, the

outdoor seating, and the walkway. We walk the path and I point to the window where his ICU room was back in February 2013. Approaching the spot where the Canada geese greeted me, Tim asks if this is where the geese were. I answer yes and we look up to the rooftop to see a few geese sitting and watching. He wants to hear the message of the geese again, so I retell the story as we make our way back to the elevator. I think I am ready to proceed to the dreaded ICU ward.

Familiar faces that remember me immediately come to grab hugs and kisses and greet us. Many of the nurses do not recall Tim right away, as he looks entirely different today from how he did a year ago. On the other hand, Shawn, Tim's physiotherapist while in the High Acuity Unit gives him a friendly handshake and congratulates my husband on a full recovery. We continue to explore the ICU ward and Tim stops to check out his room. There is a patient there today and Tim asks if he looked this way as well. I reply that indeed he looked exactly the same way this stranger does today. After making our rounds for about an hour, we finally see the good doctor. Dr. Blake also remembers me, yet can't quite pinpoint my husband's illness. I gently remind him that Tim was his Legionnaires' patient. Dr. Blake is thrilled to see Tim walking about in fine health and states he loves to see his patients return to visit, especially since there are not many that have a positive outcome like my husband's. He asks me if I had sought closure from last year's critical incident. I knew I had and it felt like my wound was finally healed.

In Mexico

My husband and I took a vacation and treated ourselves for the first time. We went to an all-inclusive Mexican vacation in Los Cabos. We enjoyed the sun kisses, the warm air, the sparkling ocean, and the soft sands. During our vacation, we decided to go on a few adventures. My husband Tim suggested one of the adventures. He booked us a day trip with a two-hour bus ride to La Paz where we would go diving with whale sharks. Tim is terrified of sharks and of swimming in the ocean, even in the calm Pacific Ocean right off the coast of British Columbia where no sharks reside. Therefore, he challenged himself to step entirely out of his comfort zone. Arriving in La Paz, we were briefed and educated by the tour guide as to what to expect during the boat trip in search of the whale shark. Once on the boat, I observed my silent husband. I was smiling as I saw pure excitement and exhilaration fill my husband's body as he relaxed. I congratulated him for making leaps and bounds and wanting to swim in this vast ocean with these magnificent creatures. We did not encounter the whale shark during this trip, yet we were not disappointed at all. We swam in the warm waters and saw marvellous wildlife and various marine mammals in their natural habitat including dolphins following the boat and performing synchronized dances for us. I could not get my husband out of the ocean that day. He conquered his fear and loved the connection to the water and its expansiveness.

On our way back to Los Cabos, we stopped in the small town of Todos Santos on the Baja Peninsula in Mexico, to visit the legendary Hotel California. In February 2013, I had imagined us dancing there.

ॐ Namaste. My soul honours your soul. I honour the place in you where the entire universe resides. I honour the light, love, truth, beauty, and peace within you, because it is also in me. In sharing these things, we are united, we are the same, we are one.

Journal Notes

Glossary

Clairaudience: The power to hear sounds said to exist beyond the reach of ordinary experience or capacity, as the voices of the dead.

Claircognizance: The ability for a person to acquire psychic knowledge without knowing how or why he or she knows it. The user can gain information about a person, object, place, or event through intrinsic knowledge; it just "comes to" the user's mind.

Clairscence or Clairalience: The ability for a person to acquire psychic knowledge by means of smelling.

Clairsentience: The power to feel beyond the physical realm; the feeling energy.

Clairvoyance: The ability to gain visual information about an object, person, location, or physical event through means other than the known human sense of seeing.

Energetic: To do with energy.

Hypnosis: A state that resembles sleep but in which you can hear and respond to questions and suggestions.

Intuition: A natural ability or power that makes it possible to know something without any proof or evidence; a feeling that guides a person to act a certain way without fully understanding why; something that is known or understood without proof or evidence.

Legionnaires' Disease: Pneumonia caused by a bacterium of the genus *Legionella* (*Legionella pneumophila*), which is characterized initially by symptoms resembling influenza (such as malaise, headache, and muscular aches) followed by high fever, cough, diarrhea, lobar pneumonia, and mental confusion. It may be fatal, especially in elderly and immunocompromised individuals.

Meditation: The act or process of spending time in quiet thought.

Mediumship: The practice of certain people—known as mediums—to purportedly mediate communication between spirits of the dead and human beings.

Near-Death Experience: A personal experience associated with impending death, and encompassing multiple possible sensations including detachment from the body, feelings of levitation, total serenity, security, warmth, the experience of absolute dissolution, and the presence of a light; or a journey to Hell.

Power Animal: A broadly animistic and shamanic concept that has entered the English language from anthropology, ethnography, and sociology. A guardian spirit guides, helps, and protects individuals, lineages, and nations. In the shamanic worldview, everything is alive, bearing an inherent virtue, power, and wisdom. In this context, power animals represent a person's connection to all life, their qualities of character, and their power.

Psychic: Used to describe strange mental powers and abilities (such as the ability to predict the future, to know what other people are thinking, or to receive messages from dead people) that cannot be explained by natural laws.

Reiki: A simple and natural healing method. It is both gentle and powerful. The power, which acts and lives in all created matter, is known as Universal Life Force.

Relaxation: A way to rest and enjoy yourself; time that you spend resting and enjoying yourself; something that you do to stop feeling nervous, worried.

Self-Sabotage: A behaviour that creates problems and interferes with goals.

Septic Shock: A life-threatening form of sepsis (a condition resulting from an infection) that usually results from the presence of gram-negative bacteria and their toxins in the bloodstream. It is characterized especially by decreased blood flow to organs and tissues, hypotension, organ dysfunction (as of the heart, kidneys, and lungs), an impaired mental state, and often multiple organ failure.

Spiritual: Relating to the spirit and to sacred things.

Stress: A state of mental tension and worry caused by problems in your life, work, etc.; something that causes strong feelings of worry or anxiety.

Synchronicities: The coincidental occurrence of events, especially psychic events (as similar thoughts in widely separated persons or a mental image of an unexpected event before it happens), that seem related but are not explained by conventional mechanisms of causality. It is used especially in the psychology of C. G. Jung.

Visualization: The formation of mental visual images; the act or process of interpreting in visual terms or of putting into visible form.

Yoga: A system of exercises for the mind and body.

REFERENCES

Books

Andrews, Ted. *Animal Speaks: The Spiritual & Magical Powers of Creatures Great and Small*

Farmer, Steven D. *Animal Spirit Guides*

Honervogt, Tanmaya. *The Complete Reiki Tutor*

Online Articles

www.articles.mercola.com/sites/articles/archive/2013/03/07/inflammation-triggers-disease-symptoms.aspx

www.news.harvard.edu/gazette/story/2006/02/meditation-found-to-increase-brain-size/chealth.canoe.ca/channel_condition_info_details.asp?disease_id=80&channel_id=1020&relation_id=71085

www.dictionary.reference.com/browse/clairaudience?s=t

www.dictionary.reference.com/browse/clairvoyance

www.en.wikipedia.org/wiki/Legionnaires'_disease

www.en.wikipedia.org/wiki/Mediumship

www.en.wikipedia.org/wiki/Power_animal

www.foodmatters.tv/
articles-1/7-health-benefits-of-meditation
greatergood.berkeley.edu/article/item/

www.tips_for_keeping_a_gratitude_journal
journal.frontiersin.org/Journal/10.3389/fpsyg.2012.00116/
abstract

www.psi.wikia.com
psychologyofwellbeing.com/201101/open-your-mind-with-
open-monitoring-meditation.html

www.active.com/fitness/
articles/7-ways-exercise-relieves-stress

www.cbc.ca/news/health/7-things-to-know-about-legion-
naires-disease-1.1134849

www.huffingtonpost.com/2013/04/08/mindfulness-medita-
tion-benefits-health_n_3016045.html

www.huffingtonpost.com/kripalu/meaning-of-
om_b_4177447.html

www.medicalnewstoday.com/articles/272833.php

www.merriam-webster.com/dictionary/synchronicity

www.psychologytoday.com/blog/use-
your-mind-change-your-brain/201305/
is-your-brain-meditation

Author Biography

 Michèle Bisson-Somerville began her corporate career as a Field Consultant with Dairy Queen Canada Inc., shortly after graduating with a degree in Political Science in her early twenties. She was awarded "Manager of the Month and Year" due to her expertise in establishing national training courses, developing business plans, managing a portfolio of franchisees with annual sales of $850,000+, generating annual sales of over $1.3 million per store, and ongoing store operation consultations.

She continued to build her business acumen through her role as a manager and trainer at Blockbuster Video Canada. During this time, she turned almost bankrupt stores into multi-million dollar establishments, once again earning her awards such as "Manager of the Quarter and Year."

At the same time, Michèle Bisson-Somerville lived with a secret identity of having an extremely flexed intuitive muscle. She decided to start using her skills by training as a Reiki Master-Teacher and attending intuitive workshops. Having achieved her goals in the corporate world, she returned to school to earn a Bachelor of Education and taught in one of Ontario's largest Francophone school districts. After teaching for one year, she moved with her family to Vancouver, British Columbia, where her gut instincts guided her to start her own business called Spiritual Ventures, which mentors men in flexing their intuitive muscles.

Knowing for quite some time that she was meant to write

a book, maybe three, it wasn't until recently that she decided that now was the time to share a bit of her story, her clients' transformations, insights from her three sons and her husband's journey in her book, *Voodoo Shit for Men—Flex your Intuitive Muscle*.

About Michèle

Personal Intuitive Trainer

Hire Michèle Bisson-Somerville

For more information on hiring Michèle Bisson-Somerville for a private mentoring or group session, email voodooshitformen@gmail.com

Websites
www.Voodooshitformen.com
www.Spiritualventures.ca

Social Media

Facebook
www.facebook.com/pages/Voodoo-Shit-for-Men/676179522472103
www.facebook.com/spiritualventures

Twitter
www.twitter.com/voodooshit4men
www.twitter.com/MichSomerville

Nutrition & Health

Be Your Best Juicy Self with Juice+
www.msomerville.canada.juiceplus.com
www.msomerville.towergarden.ca
www.michelesomerville.transform30.com

If you want to get on the path to be a published author by
Influence Publishing please go to
www.InfluencePublishing.com

Inspiring books that influence change

More information on our other titles and how to submit
your own proposal can be found at
www.InfluencePublishing.com